MW01296364

Your Call To

Freedom!

An Interactive Guidebook
With Bible-Based Tools To Heal From
An Abusive Relationship

By

Michele Ruth Jones

authorHOUSE®

AuthorHouse™
1663 Liberty Drive
Bloomington, IN 47403
www.authorhouse.com
Phone: 1 (800) 839-8640

© 2005 Michele Ruth Jones. All rights reserved.

No part of this book may be reproduced, stored in a retrieval system, or
transmitted by any means without the written permission of the author.

Published by AuthorHouse 05/02/2019

ISBN: 978-1-4184-5272-8 (sc)

Library of Congress Control Number: 2003096602

Print information available on the last page.

Any people depicted in stock imagery provided by Getty Images are models,
and such images are being used for illustrative purposes only.
Certain stock imagery © Getty Images.

This book is printed on acid-free paper.

Because of the dynamic nature of the Internet, any web addresses or links contained in
this book may have changed since publication and may no longer be valid. The views
expressed in this work are solely those of the author and do not necessarily reflect the
views of the publisher, and the publisher hereby disclaims any responsibility for them.

"Now the Lord is the Spirit, and where the Spirit of the Lord is, there is freedom."

2 Corinthians 3:17 NIV

Dedicated To

Jesus Christ–My Blessed Savior, My Provider, and My Source of Strength!

My Mother–Elaine Ruth Jones

My Maternal Grandmother–Ruth Storey

My Paternal Grandmother–Edna Jones

My Father–John Lee Jones

My Grandfather–Samuel Storey

My Brother–Gary Lee Jones

My Sister–Melissa Ruth Jones

My Nephew–Jonathan Lee Jones

My dearest friends, who prayed, cried with me and encouraged me to "press on" in the Lord! Each of your lives is a gift to this earth from God.

Margarette Pierre-Louis

Jennifer Murray

Carol Feracho

Maria Meriles

Sharon Wynn-Robles

Denise Perry-Eans

Deborah Simmons

Christine Perchell

Pamela James

I thank The Reverends Chris and Peg Rhone, and Pastor Rich Hurst for their dynamic spiritual leadership example and for stirring up the gift placed within me (2 Timothy 1:6). Jodi Taylor, Bobbie Oliver, Linda Williamson, Rae Myers, Roxanne Mills, Brian Horting, Barbara Israel and Carolyn Wheeler for their heartfelt project feedback.

Most importantly and above all, I thank my risen Lord and Savior Jesus Christ! He alone restored my broken heart, opened my "blinded" eyes and set this captive *FREE!* This soul is eternally grateful.

"For nothing is impossible with God."
Luke 1:37 NIV

Unless otherwise indicated, all Scripture quotations are taken from *The Amplified Bible* (AMP) from within The Comparative Study Bible.

The Comparative Study Bible
Copyright © 1984 by The Zondervan Corporation
Grand Rapids, Michigan 49350, U.S.A.
Library of Congress Catalog Card Number: 84-51724
All Rights Reserved

The Amplified Bible
The Amplified Bible, copyright © 1965;
The Amplified Bible, Old Testament, Part One, copyright © 1964;
The Amplified Old Testament, Part Two, copyright © 1962 by the Zondervan
    Corporation
The Amplified New Testament, copyright © 1958, 1987;
The Amplified Gospel of John, copyright © 1954,1987 by the Lockmar
    Foundation La Habra, CA 90631.
All Rights Reserved.

The New American Standard Version
New American Standard Version copyright © The Lockman Foundation
1960, 1962, 1963, 1968, 1971, 1972, 1973, 1975, 1977
A Corporation not for profit
La Habra, California
All Rights Reserved

The New International Version
The Holy Bible, New International Version
Copyright © 1973, 1978, 1984 by International Bible Society

Scripture taken from the HOLY BIBLE, NEW INTERNATIONAL
VERSION. Copyright © 1973, 1978, 1984 by International Bible Society.
Used by permission of Zondervan Publishing House. All rights reserved.

The "NIV" and "New International Version" trademarks are registered in the
United States Patent and Trademark Office by International Bible Society.
Use of either trademark requires permission of International Bible Society.

Printed in the United States of America

96 97 98 99 15 14 13 12

The Message; The New Testament, Psalms and Proverbs
Copyright © 1993, 1994, 1995 by Eugene H. Peterson. Used by permission of
NavPress Publishing Group.

Words emphasized by the author in Scripture quotations are underlined or in bold face. This emphasis does not appear in the original source of the Scripture quotations.

Contents

Keys To Freedom

Closing Notes

Jacqueline —
You are Father's Masterpiece
He's calling you to rise
And SHINE for His
glory & He's got your
back ♡
Blessings
Coach Michele

Introduction

To Whom This Interactive Guidebook Is Written

To you who have cried countless times and nights into tear-stained pillows.

To you who are smiling on the outside, yet emotionally hemorrhaging on the inside.

To you who slips away from her desk during the day to cry privately in the restroom or in your car.

To you who wonder if God cares or is beginning to believe He has forgotten you.

Today I'm here to let you personally know…

He sees your tears, wants to wipe your eyes and His heart grieves with you.

There IS HOPE…you are NOT alone!

Today, know the Lord wants to dry your eyes. He directed you to this book as a witness that He dearly loves you and desires to free you from pain and fear.

> *"I sought (inquired of) for the Lord and required Him [of necessity, and on the authority of His Word], and He <u>heard</u> me, and <u>delivered</u> me from all my fears."*
> Psalms 34:4

God cares about the quality and faithfulness of your marital relationship. His heart grieves when one spouse mistreats the other. He desires for us <u>not</u> to use "empty words," <u>but</u> to change our ways, correct our behaviors (repent), and return to Him.

> *"Yet you ask, Why does He reject it? Because the Lord was witness [to the covenant made at your marriage] between you and the wife of your youth, against whom you have dealt treacherously <u>and</u> to whom you were faithless. Yet she is your companion and the wife of your covenant [made by your marriage vows].*
>
> *And did not God make [you and your wife] one [flesh]? Did not One make you and preserve your spirit alive? And why did God make you two one? Because He sought a godly offspring [from your union]. Therefore <u>take heed to yourselves, and let no one deal treacherously and be faithless to the wife of his youth.</u>*
>
> *For the Lord, the God of Israel, says: I <u>hate divorce and marital separation, and him who covers his garment [his wife] with violence.</u> Therefore keep a watch upon your spirit [that it may be controlled by My Spirit], that <u>you deal not treacherously and faithlessly [with your marriage mate].</u>*
>
> *You have wearied the Lord with your words. Yet you say, In what way have we wearied Him? [You do it when by your actions] you say, Everyone who does evil is good in the sight of the Lord, and He delights in them. Or [by asking], where is the God of justice?"*
> Malachi 2:14-17

2

Is Your Wing Broken?

Your wing is the dream or vision in your heart that you longed for, anticipated, and awaited.

Your wing is the vision you thought would take you onward and upward in your life.

Your wing, so you thought, would fulfill your life's dreams.

Yet instead of taking you upward, something goes terribly wrong. Your wing becomes "broken" and sadly now confines you to the ground, with no hope of flying upward unless it is restored.

In this interactive guidebook you will travel from the brokenness of my wing, through the restoration process, and my eventual, upward calling to healing and true freedom through Jesus Christ!

My wing broke and became crushed after being separated multiple times from my spouse. He chose to ultimately abandon me and I eventually chose to divorce him to leave an emotionally abusive marriage.

My trials ranged from loss of self, declining self-esteem, depression, isolation, thoughts of suicide, then anger with the Church, God, and myself. Yet the Lord's kindness and compassion drew me back. The healing started when I took the time to stop, humble myself before Jesus Christ, and cry out to Him.

Just know that He has an answer of peace for you today! This is **your** call to freedom! Will you answer it?

> *"The Lord is close to those who are of a broken heart, and saves such as are crushed with sorrow for sin and are humbly and thoroughly penitent."*
> Psalms 34:18

Purpose of This Interactive Guidebook

"There is a way which seems right to a man and appears straight before him, but at the end of it are the ways of death."
Proverbs 14:12

It is only the Lord who knows the right way and He ALONE who can shed light on your dark and confusing path.

I am sharing with you the series of humbling YET challenging truths revealed to me these past few years that healed and restored my shattered heart and mind from an abusive marriage.

The Lord *is not a respecter* of persons, and what He has done for me, He will do for you.

The sole intent of this book is to shed light onto your dark path, offer comfort for a distressing season of life and provide *hope*, because no situation is impossible when you follow the prompting of the Lord Jesus Christ!

Abuse can be defined as "abnormal use of the original intended purpose."

Abuse comes in many forms: mental, emotional, verbal, destruction of personal property, sexual and physical. Regardless of the method, the devastating effects are still the same. As a result of domestic abuse, the heart, mind, and inner soul become wounded.

Similar to when you are afflicted with a physical wound, your heart and soul builds up "scar tissue" to protect you if the violating behavior continues. In an attempt at self preservation, sadly <u>you too</u> become "calloused" in your heart.

With physical wounds, the healing process involves opening the calloused/scarred area then cleansing out the original wound, so <u>fresh</u>

new tissue may emerge. During the cleansing phase, sometimes the rinsing wash stings as the toxins flush away.

As you journey with this guidebook, the inner wounds of your heart will be reopened, then cleansed with the "water" of God's Word so you may enjoy <u>fresh</u> new inner tissue of the soul and heart. You **too** may experience some inner "stings" as the toxins in your heart and soul are rinsed away. Yet, to genuinely overcome, "rinsing" is a necessary part of the healing process!

This guidebook will enlighten you, comfort your heart by letting you know the Lord desires for you to be healed and FREE (emotionally, mentally, and spiritually)!

Yes, you **can** be healed from the inside out!

This book is for those who genuinely desire to move from VICTIM to VICTOR from BROKENNESS to WHOLENESS from BONDAGE to FREEDOM!

What can you expect by actively reading this guidebook and taking the restoration journey?

- You'll find proven keys to unlock your prison door and how to step out into His marvelous light and freedom!

- You will be challenged as I was challenged in exercising my power of choice! Choice in your thought life, choice in your speaking pattern, choice in your attitude, and choice in your actions. If you are like me, I had given up my power of choice and was allowing life to happen to me (reactively) instead of acting proactively.

- You will discover HOW to begin exercising your power of "free will" choice. As you develop a stronger muscle of choice, you will begin making quality choices.

- You will be challenged with new information or reminded of former information.

- You will be "washed" in the medicinal cleanser of the Word of God.

What is the best way to use this guidebook?

The truths revealed in this guidebook are not to condemn, but to enlighten you in moving towards healing, restoration, and change!

Section 1 of the book lays out the Biblical foundation of domestic abuse and instructs you how to best prepare for your journey to overcome the devastating effects of abuse. In **Section 2** of the book, "Keys To Freedom," you will find eleven Keys. At the end of each Freedom Key chapter you will find:

✔ **Quality Choice** – God's perspective

✔ **Prescription** – Scriptural truths to apply

✔ **Practical Exercises** – Actions to apply

As you continue and follow through to the Closing Notes, you will change! Yes, you will feel uncomfortable at times, but growth and change are for our advancement in life.

Each Freedom Key builds upon the next. You will want to read accordingly. As you discover a Freedom Key, digest it, reflect upon it, and then choose to act on it accordingly.

Each Freedom Key is a separate area of study allowing you to pause and reflect on your specific areas of need.

Today, make a quality decision with the goal of healing to challenge yourself to commit to this guidebook for the next twelve weeks! During this time determine that the focus will be on you! Lay aside any other "time stealers" or distractions such as television, other reading materials or "busy work". This allows you ample guarded time to read and reflect about your life with the presented Scriptures.

As you commit to each Key with a serious desire to overcome, you will achieve results.

Enjoy yourself! Keep this guidebook on your night table, in your handbag, or in the car and take your time in reading and savoring each nourishing truth.

You are not alone. Seek the Lord and allow Him to gently guide you through each Key.

This book will not advise you whether or not to divorce. That is a prayerful and personal decision between you, your spiritual elders, and the Holy Spirit.

> *"Our inner selves wait [earnestly] for the Lord; He is our help and our shield"*
> Psalms 33:20

Prescription

1. God sent His Word to heal and deliver you from the depth of any pit, choose to take His hand.
   Psalms 34:17,18; Psalms 107:20

2. God can <u>and</u> desires to heal the innermost wounds of your heart. Will you allow Him?
   Psalms 147:3

3. You are not an outcast or a forsaken woman! At this moment the Lord is actively pursuing you. Today, He wants to heal and strengthen you.
   Jeremiah 30:17; Ezekiel 34:15,16

4. The Lord will repay you, restore back to you the years that were lost, and stolen from you due to abuse.
   Joel 2:25

"Mirror Mirror on the Wall:" What Is the Truth About Marriage... Is Your Mirror Foggy?

What helped you form your earliest impressions of marriage? For most of us, it is the example of our parents' marriage. Their actions framed our definitions of the male-female, wife-husband roles. Many women carry a "fantasy image" sketched by magazines, books, movies, or sometimes soap opera story lines. In each of those avenues, the characters marry and "live happily ever after." Has anyone ever gone behind the scenes to see what "happily ever after" looked like?

God designed marriage to be honorable. The marital bed is holy and intended for a whole man and a whole woman to mutually honor, care, and submit to one another.

> *"Let marriage be held in honor—esteemed worthy, precious, [that is,] of great price and especially dear—in all things. And thus let the marriage bed be (kept undishonored,) undefiled."*
> Hebrews 13:4a

> *"He who finds a [true] wife finds a good thing, and obtains favor of the Lord."*
> Proverbs 18:22

> *"Be subject to one another out of reverence for Christ, the Messiah, the Anointed One."*
> Ephesians 5:21

Without an accurate or clear understanding of God's plan for marriage, we behave in ways "we think or believe" are appropriate.

> *"For not knowing about God's righteousness, and <u>seeking to establish their own</u>, they did not subject themselves to the righteousness of God."*
> Romans 10:3 NAS

I was married at 33. Up to that moment, my life included traveling, endeavoring to grow personally and in my uniqueness as a single Christian woman. I actively participated in the church, pursued the things of God for almost ten years prior and led a weekly home Bible study group. I worked hard and with the grace of God became quite successful in the corporate world, having access to company cars, extravagant expense accounts, and traveling in first-rate accommodations.

Eighteen months before meeting my future mate, I purchased my first home and excitedly looked forward to the prospect of decorating it. Two months after I moved into the home, my future husband and I met at a local hardware store. We were introduced at the checkout counter by a mutual acquaintance that happened to be working at the store that particular day.

This planted the seed for a budding friendship. Over the next three months, we became inseparable. I enjoyed his sense of humor and relaxed style while he enjoyed my candid approach to life.

As time passed I trusted him to dog-sit for me and he would buy emergency groceries for me when I traveled so I'd return home to a stocked house.

One day he asked to join me in attending church. This became a regular activity, he would pick me up on Sundays for church, and then we'd spend the afternoon at lunch or visiting with other singles from the church. He traveled with me on special company-sponsored events. He became my dear friend and companion.

We got married in the fall of the following year, in a lovely ceremony and lively reception of friends and family. We danced and celebrated until the early morning hours.

We went on a tropical honeymoon, yet it was during the second evening of the honeymoon that our relationship began to change.

We were discussing how we planned to handle joint household responsibilities when we returned home from the trip. He shared how he'd been experiencing some pain and physical discomfort from his current job. I asked him if he would consider changing professions.

He became enraged, cursed at me, walked away, and then barely said two sentences to me during dinner. That evening he refused to allow me to touch him as he grabbed the sheets and turned his shoulder to me in bed. I had no idea this behavior could or would repeat itself and escalate from this point.

The next few years became a pattern of good days, followed by days when he felt offended and "punished" me by not speaking to me. He would leave the house for days at a time without telling me where he was going and tell me if I wanted to contact him, I'd have to call his pager. After these episodes I'd apologize, then he would respond with a card and flowers. This became a destructive "dance cycle" that grew more frequent. Our core issues were questions on intimacy—I wanted to know why he couldn't or wouldn't treat me in a wifely manner and each time his response was "you're becoming too needy or that's just not me." After we were married the affection level suddenly began to drop. Yet while he courted me, showing affection or simple handholding was not a concern.

With a burning desire to maintain our marriage, I was receptive to doing whatever was necessary to please him. I went on a quest to lose weight, began working out, changed my hairstyle, and even changed mannerisms to become whatever woman he needed.

He initially refused counseling, so I began marital counseling on my own. I tried to discover how to become a better wife, how to change my personality, and how to be willing to do whatever he asked me to do.

During our third separation, he contacted me, severely sick with the flu, and asked me to bring him home. (I had no idea where he had been staying the past two weeks.) When he gave me the address I was shocked. It was less than two miles away from our home meaning he had to drive past our house to go to and from work each day!

I picked him up, helped him change and stayed by the shower to make sure he didn't fall. Afterwards, I helped him get into bed.

The next two days I fed him soup and he cuddled under me while he slept. On the third day I returned home from work. The house was quiet, so I crept in slowly so I wouldn't disturb him. I walked into the bedroom to find the bed neatly made with no sign of him anywhere.

I looked in his den, the kitchen, and then spotted a note on the dining room table. It read, "Thanks, feeling better, went back to my buddy's home." I was devastated. I sat there in shock and cried; I balled up the note and threw it across the room.

It finally clicked in my head. He had no desire to respect our marriage vows or to work through our problems.

I slowly took off my clothes. All the energy drained from my bones from crying. I changed into my nightgown and crawled into bed. I stayed there for two days, feeling numb and hopeless. I felt helpless and cornered in with no place to go and no hope for change in sight.

After much prayer and crying out to the Lord for direction, He revealed that if I continued in this same behavioral "dance pattern" with my husband, I would eventually die. First I would die from the inside (my heart and soul withering), and then I would die mentally and physically from the inner brokenness. The edges of my heart had already become gray and brittle, so this image of me dying from the inside out spoke volumes to me. Yet I ignored it, thinking, "it will be okay, I'll turn the other cheek again."

I alone again sought marital counseling with our pastor and his wife. Eventually my husband joined the counseling. Our relationship did begin to revive once we both agreed to get back on track according to God's instruction and jointly work on mutual concerns.

Sadly, less than six months later, our "cyclical" behaviors returned and the separations began again.

During this final separation, I shared that I would reconcile only if he found the counselor he approved, and I would abide by the counselor's instruction. Previously, he had stated that the former pastor was "on my side and he would not objectively hear him." Within a month, he found a male Christian counselor who met all of his criteria.

We met with the counselor on three separate occasions and his final evaluation was the same as our previous counselors. My husband was unwilling to accept the guidance or to make changes and I was unwilling to live in that condition of emotional cruelty for the rest of my life.

During our final year of marriage, my husband only allowed me to contact him by way of his pager. Discussions for any further steps to save our marriage would be under his terms only and not from the terms of the various counselors.

Separated again and with no mutual desire for change, I weighed the matter in prayer with further spiritual counsel. I took account of my remaining "threads" of self-respect and sanity, and notified him of my decision to file for divorce.

I shared that I was unable to continue a marriage union under these conditions and from that point he made no further attempts for reconciliation. Even on the final day of the divorce proceeding, I waited outside of the courtroom for him to appear, anxiously hoping for any glimmer of reconciliation. Yet he chose not to appear.

My "wing" of hopes and dreams was now broken. It was now totally crushed and I saw no hope of healing for my disappointed heart.

Getting to the Root of the Matter: The Spiritual Dynamics of Abuse

"My people are destroyed for lack of knowledge…"
Hosea 4:6

This chapter is devoted to explaining the various faces of domestic abuse as well as sharing God's original plan for marriage and mankind's way of marriage.

Types of Domestic Abuse

- Emotional

- Psychological

- Verbal

- Sexual

- Property Destruction

- Physical

Most people primarily equate domestic abuse with physical domination and control. Yet the other forms of abuse are just as devastating! Why? Because physical wounds can be seen **and** do heal… but, the UNSEEN, inflicted, inward wounds to the heart and soul from the other forms of abuse can last a **lifetime** unless they are effectively addressed and healed!

I recall as a little girl, the words we used to say to each other in the schoolyard: "Sticks and stones may break my bones, yet names will NEVER hurt me!"…Well, that is FALSE according to the truths of Scripture and you too may personally know the damaging inner effects of negative words.

*"Death and life are in the power of the tongue, and they
who indulge it shall eat the fruit of it [for death or life]."*
Proverbs 18:21

Words have an inherent power to build you up or to tear you down.
The deceptively insidious nature of the other forms of domestic abuse
is that since "inward" wounds cannot be seen, the outside world
mistakenly thinks you are "okay". Yet, **you know** on the inside you are
in pain or, in some cases, "hemorrhaging" in your heart and soul.
Without effective treatment to the inner wounds, the damaging effects
grow worse.

God's Plan for Marriage

*"In the same way you married men should live considerately
with [your wives], with an intelligent recognition [of the
marriage relation], honoring the woman as [physically] the
weaker, but [realizing that you] are joint heirs of the grace
(God's unmerited favor) of life, in order that your prayers
may not be hindered and cut off.—Otherwise you cannot
pray effectively.*

*Finally, all [of you] should be of one and the same mind
(united in spirit), sympathizing [with one another], loving
[each the others] as brethren (of one household), compassionate
and courteous-tenderhearted and humble-minded."*
I Peter 3:7,8

Jesus Christ shared these truths:

We error when we do not know the Scriptures or the power of God
(Matthew 22:29). Our choice to follow traditions will make the Word of
God of no effect (Matthew 15:3). We at times choose to give our
traditions more importance than the Word of God (Mark 7:9).

As you continue, here's your challenge: what traditions or
preconceived ideas about marriage and male/female roles do you
maintain?

God's perspective records the following truth:

- Mutual submission, care and concern.
  Ephesians 5:21,23,25

- Both hold mutual value and worth in God's eyes.
  Galatians 3:27-29; Genesis 5:2

- Both are created in His image/both with dominion.
  Genesis 1:27,28; Colossians 3:9,10

- Both are given mutual conjugal authority
  1 Corinthians 1:1-5

- Both are heirs of God's unmerited favor
  1 Peter 3:7

God's marital plan outlined in the Scriptures specifically records the boundaries, the roles and responsibilities for each party. When the husband and wife *each* operate within their God given roles and responsibilities the plan works! Living in a large metropolitan area, I use the analogy of a "super highway" to describe the clear boundary lanes God has given to both the husband and the wife. I've realized, when I "stay in my lane" as I drive on the highway, each time I arrive at my destination safe and sound. In contrast, if I swerve into someone else's lane or another driver attempts to aggressively "cut into" to my lane, this creates unnecessary confusion or the risk of extreme danger for all parties involved. Accordingly from the Scriptures the husband and wife must learn to **"stay in their respective lane"** for their relationship to safely travel to a good destination!

Let us begin discovering God's orderly plan for marriage:

God's Plan / Non-Violence Wheel

- The Non-Violence Wheel Offers a view of a GODLY, HEALTHY relationship based on equality and non-violence.

- The Non-Violence Wheel is also helpful in setting goals and boundaries in a marital relationship.

- The Book of Genesis defines God's original plan for marriage as a <u>mutually</u> respectful, trusting and loving relationship.

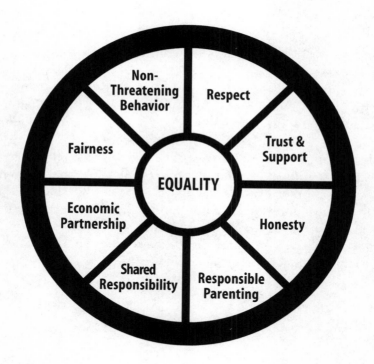

(Adapted from Peace At Home (formerly Battered Women Fighting Back), Boston; ph 617.482.9497; fax 617.482.6504).

Mankind's Handling of Marriage

Before the downfall of Adam and Eve, they enjoyed a mutually loving, vibrant, and honest marital relationship.

> *"Therefore a man shall leave his father and his mother and shall become united and cleave to his wife, and they shall become one flesh.*
>
> *And the man and his wife were both naked, and were <u>not</u> embarrassed or ashamed in each other's presence."*
> Genesis 2:24,25

The Hebrew words[1] explain the depth of the intimacy and openness of Adam and Eve's union. The couple freely enjoyed an open, honest and transparent relationship with one another. The original marriage relationship included FREEDOM from fear, shame, or disgrace.

Naked is *"arom,"* meaning without clothing or stripped of outer or peculiar garment <u>designating</u> rank or office.

Ashamed is *"bosh,"* which means to feel shame, the type of internal shame that sometimes may or ought to prevent an action. With the use of "not" this means Adam and Eve enjoyed a marital relationship that was <u>free</u> of stereotypes, guilt, shame or any inclination to draw back from one another!

By <u>mutual</u> poor choice, Adam and Eve shared in the downfall of mankind. Eve, being deceived by the serpent, chose to eat of the forbidden fruit and offered it to her husband (Genesis 3:13). Adam knowingly chose to disobey God by choosing to follow his wife's prompting (1 Timothy 2: 14). Both refused to accept responsibility and accountability for their choices.

Their choices by free will brought the consequences of sin into the world. From that moment the relationship between God and mankind died, while the relationship between husband and wife eroded.

Behaviors and Consequences of Sin

As recorded in Genesis chapter 3:

- Covering yourself up – Genesis 3:7

- Hiding from the presence of God – Genesis 3:8

- Fear and sense of shame (loss of freedom) – Genesis 3:10

- Choosing to take advice of others over the Word of God – Genesis 3:11

- Adam blames God for the choice **he** exercised – Genesis 3:12

- Eve blames the serpent for her choice – Genesis 3:13

- God informs Eve she will now have a craving and desire for her husband. (Previously her desire was rooted in her relationship with God) – Genesis 3:16

- God informs Eve that the reporting order now changes. Her husband will now have headship over her. – Genesis 3:16

Behaviors of blaming others, excusing, justifying, rationalizing, and even blaming God for one's poor choice to disobey His instruction now entered into mankind's lifestyle.

Man's Plan / Violence Wheel

- This wheel helps link the different SINFUL behaviors that together form a pattern of abuse. You see the relationship as a whole - and how each seemingly unrelated behavior is an important part in an overall effort to <u>control</u> someone.
- ABUSE = Abnormal use of the originally intended purpose.
- The Bible clearly records that these <u>DEVIANT</u> natures entered the world after the "fall of mankind" in the Garden of Eden.

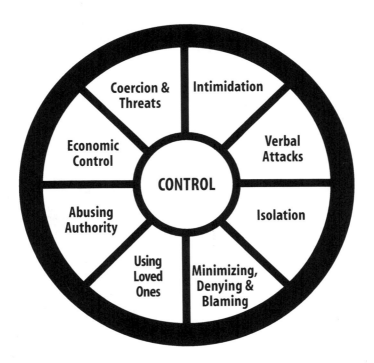

(Adapted from Peace At Home (formerly Battered Women Fighting Back), Boston; ph 617.482.9497; fax 617.482.6504).

In mankind's plan for marriage, the motivating factor of domestic abuse is a need to "control" someone else and the marriage relationship.

God never instructs or gives us the authority to "control" anyone. Instead, we are instructed repeatedly throughout the Scriptures to exercise SELF-CONTROL and SELF-DISCIPLINE.

If you have wrongfully allowed someone to "control" you or "override into your personal lane," the tools in this guidebook will enhance your self-control and teach you <u>how</u> to exercise your God given boundaries.

The Dance of Destruction

There is a three-step "dance," a behavioral pattern, which keeps the destructive cycle in motion. It can only be broken once the misbehaviors are clearly identified and its working dynamics are recognized.

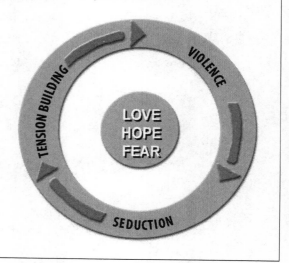

"Dance of Destruction"/Cycle of Violence

- These actions often become a flawed 3-step behavioral "dance" pattern within the home.

- **T**ension Building
  Violence
  Seduction

- Often the "dance" increases with intensity and frequency.

LOVE
HOPE
FEAR

TENSION BUILDING

VIOLENCE

SEDUCTION

(Adapted from Peace At Home (formerly Battered Women Fighting Back), Boston; ph 617.482.9497; fax 617.482.6504).

The Cycle of Violence shows these actions become inappropriate behavioral patterns, which operate in three phases:

Phase 1 - Tension Building: includes criticism, yelling, swearing, using angry gestures, blaming, accusations, coercion, and threats.

Phase 2 - Violence: includes verbal assaults, physical and sexual attacks and threats.

Phase 3 - Seduction: includes apologizing, promises to change, and gifts.

It also explains how three dynamics of thought—love, hope and fear—keep the cycle in motion, making it challenging to correct an abusive relationship.

- Love: for your partner, thinking the relationship has its good points; "it's not all bad."

- Hope: the behaviors will change; "the relationship didn't begin like this."

- Fear: the threats to harm you or your family will become a reality, and fear of confrontation because **you** are afraid of "being alone" or rejected.

Without the proper instruction and a willingness to change you are destined to repeat the same behavioral patterns. Studies have shown children raised in abusive homes often model the witnessed behaviors. Boys will have the tendency to become abusive mates while the girls will grow up to marry an abusive mate. You can make a quality choice today to end the cycle!

God's original plan for marriage is available today to those who choose to apply His healing and life changing truths.

6

Choose to Get on the Road to Freedom

When you reach a point where the inner hurt and pain are too much to bear, choose to cry out to Jesus Christ, "Help me Lord! I need you!"

When you ask the Lord with an attitude of confidence, trust and EXPECTANCY, He hears you.

> *"...all things can be—are possible—to him who believes!"*
> Mark 9:23

Receive Your Healing

Jesus Christ came to heal you and to set you free from all bondage—mental, emotional, physical, and spiritual! (Isaiah 61:1).

> *"And Jesus went about all the cities and villages, teaching in their synagogues and proclaiming the good news (the Gospel) of the kingdom, and curing all kinds of disease and every weakness and infirmity.*
>
> *When He saw the throngs, He was moved with pity and sympathy for them, because they were bewildered—harassed and distressed and dejected and helpless—like sheep without a shepherd."*
> Matthew 9:35,36

Here are some records of men and women who seriously desired healing. Each cried out to Jesus Christ and believed He could heal them. Each received healing **according to their expectation.**

After each Scripture passage you will see the "key action" word that impacted the person's healing.

- **The Woman with the Twelve-year-old Issue (Mark 5:24-34)**

Sometimes you have had your "issue" for so long and sadly used all your financial and emotional resources in search of an answer. This woman spent her entire income searching for recovery the world's way. Jesus Christ told her "**your** believing, **your** expectancy" has made **you** whole.

FAITH (believing) = firm persuasion, conviction[1]

Many may be hurting, yet it is **the most desperate ones** who will choose to grasp for healing towards GENUINE wholeness. In each recorded healing, their faith was based solely upon hearing the Word of the Lord.

Each person that received healing held a relying confidence in what they heard from Jesus Christ, they chose not to be limited by the reality of their circumstances. This truth works the same way today too! The question is do you trust Him and will you receive His Word of truth?

- **The Invalid of Thirty-eight Years (John 5:2-14)**

Sometimes we become "invalids" by not exercising our free will! We inactively lie in a perceived helpless condition, allowing life to "happen" to us. We become a "victim" in our own minds.

Jesus Christ is also asking you today... **"Do you want to become well? Are you really earnest about getting well?"**

WILL = to wish, desire, implying the simple act of volition[1]

- **The Blind Beggar (Mark 10:46-52; Luke 18:35-42)**

The man's targeted goal was made known to Jesus Christ and the man received his request. There are times in life when you are "blind" and cannot clearly find your way.

Jesus Christ is also asking you today, **"What do YOU want Me to do for you?"** As the blind beggar, you **too** must boldly state your need, and then receive your answer.

RECEIVE = to take from anyone, to receive with the idea of completeness, to receive in full[1]

- ## The Woman "Crippled" for Eighteen Years (Luke 13:11-17)

You may be in the same condition as this woman; your life is "crippled, bowed over, restricted" by satanic spirits. Sadly this woman was unable to make human eye contact, nor enjoy her life because of her eighteen-year-old condition. Jesus Christ saw the true nature of her situation and had compassion for the woman. He understood her pain and shame.

Jesus Christ also understands your shame; He declares to you today, **"Woman, <u>you are set free</u> from your infirmity!"**

INFIRMITY = feebleness, weakness, lack of strength, or sickness[1]

- ## The Lunatic Boy Possessed from Childhood (Mark 9:17-24)

Your situation started in childhood and it still negatively controls your life. Often the lunatic boy's condition would bring him harm by throwing the boy into fires during seizures. Your "sick situation" may also bring harm to you and distress to your family members who are helplessly watching.

Jesus Christ shared that **all things are possible to those who believe in His Word.** And the boy was healed according to the father's belief on behalf of the son.

BELIEVE = be persuaded, to rely upon, to trust, a self-surrendering fellowship; a fully assured and unswerving confidence[1]

UNBELIEF = Faithlessness, untrustworthy; distrust[1]

God desires to pour blessings on you...will YOU choose to receive?

"Yet the Lord longs to be gracious to you; he rises to show you compassion. For the Lord is a God of justice. Blessed are all who wait for him!"
Isaiah 30:18 NIV

God REWARDS those who diligently seek Him.

> *"But without faith it is impossible to please and be satisfactory to Him. For whoever would come near to God must (necessarily) believe that God exists and that He is a Rewarder of those who earnestly and diligently seek Him (out)."*
> Hebrews 11:6

Eternal Keys to Healing

To receive your healing from God, you must recognize and accept these eternal truths. Your healing is:

- According to YOUR faith in God's spoken Word... the specific promise for your need.

- According to your willingness/expectancy to receive.

- According to your determination and commitment to receive the promise.

- According to your obedience to the instruction Christ gives.

Finally, Christ desires that once you receive your deliverance/healing – you are to continue in your blessing by doing the right thing. (John 5:14 "Stop missing the mark.")

7

How to Prepare for Your Freedom Journey

The Gift…will you receive it?

Every trip requires equipment to successfully enjoy the adventure. Equipment required for this trip comes in a large, yet FREE gift box!

The gift includes God's *grace* and His *righteousness.* Without accepting the gift, you cannot successfully move forward on your journey.

An acronym for grace:

God's **R**iches **A**t **C**hrist's **E**xpense

Righteousness, a free gift from God, also includes personally knowing you now have <u>right standing</u> with God because of your relationship with Jesus Christ. You can now come boldly before the presence of God, without any sense of shame, guilt or condemnation! What a privilege, and yes it is ***FREE!***

Grace is <u>God's</u> enablement given to you to accomplish His will for your life.

God gave you the GIFT of grace and righteousness to successfully navigate in this life. You will need to ask God for His support and encouragement as you move forward in this cleansing and healing process.

How To Receive YOUR Healing!

"But God's free gift is not at all to be compared to the trespass—His grace is out of all proportion to the fall of man. For if many died through one man's falling away—his lapse, his offense—much more profusely did God's grace and the free gift [that comes] through the undeserved favor of the one Man Jesus Christ, abound and overflow to and for [the benefit of] many."
Romans 5:15

To RECEIVE healing you must first recognize that it is a GIFT (a free gift!) from God and you always have the choice to accept it or reject it.

As Christians, we usually hinder ourselves from receiving God's gift when we fail to realize it's a two-part equation. We usually walk away before doing our part (which is receiving).

A + B = C

A – You ask God; He responds

B – You make a choice to receive/accept from God

C – Your joy is full

> *"Up to this time, you have not asked a [single] thing in My name [that is, presenting all I AM] but now ask and keep on asking and you will receive, so that your joy (gladness, delight) may be full and complete."*
> John 16:24

You are to ASK God for your desired healing… and then EXPECT to receive, so that <u>your</u> joy may be full!

The grace of God was upon Jesus Christ, upon the twelve apostles and <u>is upon you</u> today.

> *"But He said to me, My grace—My favor and loving-kindness and mercy—are enough for you, [that is, sufficient against any danger and to enable you to bear the trouble manfully]; for <u>My strength and power are made perfect—fulfilled and completed and show themselves most effective—in [your] weaknesses.</u> Therefore, I will all the more gladly glory in my weaknesses and infirmities, that the strength and power of Christ, the Messiah, may rest-yes, may pitch a tent [over] and dwell-upon me!"*
> 2 Corinthians 12:9

Grace is <u>His power</u> that gives you supernatural ease, confidence and the ability to victoriously go through anything which God instructs you to do.

You must be willing to realize that within yourself you cannot accomplish or endure anything!

That's the sole reason you must use the FREE GIFT of the grace of God to help you move forward.

Please say this prayer, inviting the Lord to strengthen you and pour out His grace upon you...

"Lord I recognize that I can do nothing through my own strength, yet through the power of Jesus Christ and with the gift of your grace and the gift of righteousness, I ask your help in this healing process. Whatever you tell me to do, I know you will give me the grace to victoriously accomplish it. Teach me to receive from you and to **not** reject **or** push away your good plan for my life. I receive and accept your healing today. I thank you for this in the name of Jesus Christ, Amen."

Are you ready to begin your journey? Grab and hold fast to your GIFT, now let's begin...

Your Personal Tour Guide: The Holy Spirit

When you travel to unknown places, it is best to take a Tour Guide. An experienced tour guide knows the terrain and will safely lead you through the rocks and jagged trails to the other side.

We cannot undergo successful healing within our personal strength; we are not equipped to handle the enormity or the depth of the task by ourselves.

For your freedom journey to be a success, you must rely upon the Holy Spirit as your personal tour guide. Before you can entrust yourself to your tour guide, you must know His qualifications and background.

• He will guide you into *truth about yourself* and your life.

> *"But when He, the Spirit of Truth (the truth-giving Spirit) comes, He will guide you into all truth—the whole, full truth. For He will not speak His own message—on His own authority—but He will tell whatever He hears [from the Father, He will give the message that has been given to Him] and He will announce and declare to you things that are to come—that will happen in the future.*
>
> *He will honor and glorify Me, because He will take of (receive, draw upon) what is Mine and will reveal (declare, disclose, transmit) it to you."*
> John 16:13,14

The Holy Spirit can and will show you the root cause of your choices and your behavior. On my freedom journey, it was revealed that I had an "enabler" and a "rescuer" personality within my marriage. As the eldest child in a "high performance" family, I apparently developed those behaviors early on and those corresponding thought patterns continued into the marriage. These tendencies caused me to excuse, justify, and not

33

confront inappropriate behaviors. The root cause is the fear of rejection and the fear of losing the love of the other party. The Holy Spirit reminded me of instances as a young child and as a wife when I exhibited the same wrong choice pattern. I wept bitterly when it was revealed, yet it became a tremendous source of spiritual growth and self-awareness.

• He will comfort and strengthen you during the journey.

> *"But the Comforter (Counselor, Helper, Intercessor, Advocate, Strengthener, Standby), the Holy Spirit, Whom the Father will send in My name [in My place, to represent Me and act on My behalf], He will teach you all things. And He will cause you to recall—will remind you of, bring to your remembrance—everything I have told you."*
> John 14:26

In genuine healing, the only way out **IS** to go through… You cannot avoid the issues or "storms of life" and be free. Going **through** into YOUR promised land from the Lord includes: acknowledging the past, letting go of old issues, confronting issues as presented, and becoming "naked" or transparent with Jesus Christ.

There is nothing harder than staying in bondage due to double-mindedness, where your mind is pulled in two opposing directions. One minute you think "yes," the next minute you think "no" about your choice. Scripture records that this only brings pain and torment to your life until you make a decision. You will only receive from God once you have made up your mind to trust Him, then you are to act upon His instruction.

> *"Only it must be in faith that he asks, with no wavering— no hesitating, no doubting. For the one who wavers (hesitates, doubts) is like the billowing surge out at sea, that is blown hither and thither and tossed by the wind.*
>
> *For truly, let not such a person imagine that he will receive anything [he asks for] from the Lord,*
>
> *[For being as he is] a man of two minds—hesitating, dubious, irresolute—[he is] unstable and unreliable and uncertain about everything (he thinks, feels, decides)."*
> James 1:6-8

Remember the Israelites in the wilderness: as long as they stayed double-minded, went "back and forth" in their minds, it extended their journey into their Promised Land! (Deuteronomy1:2, 2:7)

Instead of entering their destination in eleven days, it took the Israelites **forty years**. Although God wanted **the best** for their lives, they refused to make quality choices and refused **to continue** on the path of making quality choices. They refused to listen to God's caring instruction.

In contrast, here's a point of encouragement to consider, Jesus Christ spent only **forty <u>days</u>** in the wilderness! We can each take a lesson from His success strategy.

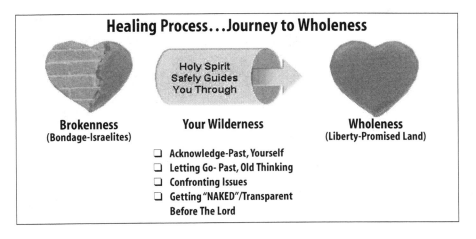

Healing Process…Journey to Wholeness

Brokenness
(Bondage-Israelites)

Your Wilderness

❑ **Acknowledge-Past, Yourself**
❑ **Letting Go- Past, Old Thinking**
❑ **Confronting Issues**
❑ **Getting "NAKED"/Transparent**
Before The Lord

Wholeness
(Liberty-Promised Land)

"When you pass through the waters I will be with you, and through the rivers they shall not overwhelm you; when you walk through the fire you shall not be burned or scorched, nor shall the flame kindle upon you."
Isaiah 43:2

I assure you the Holy Spirit is here to safely walk you through your wilderness valley, yet you must make a choice to step forward and follow His prompting.

I Corinthians 10:1-11 does forewarn us of specific attitudes and behaviors to become aware of and accept that they are counterproductive to promoting healing. Why? These same attitudes will also extend your timeframe in your wilderness valley if you choose to allow them. The following attitudes caused the Israelites to waste forty years in reaching the Promised Land, a destination that is only an **eleven day distance from their starting point!**

Attitudes and behaviors that delay your healing:

• An unbelieving/faithless attitude

• A murmuring/complaining/backbiting attitude

• Idolatry, worshipping other gods before God Almighty

• Sexual Sin

The Lord desires to do a NEW THING in your life starting today! Will you allow Him?

As you journey with this guidebook, your original wounds will be cleansed as you cooperate in the process. This book and the guidance of the Holy Spirit will lead you into all truth about your life and set you free!

Decide today to allow the Holy Spirit to tenderly take your hand and kindly guide you on your journey.

If you don't know Him, I urge you right now to ask Him into your heart.

"Jesus, I confess you now as my Lord and Savior. I ask you to come into my heart;

I believe God raised you from the dead to save me from my sins and all the consequences of sin.

I thank you; I am yours.

I also thank you for and I accept the gift of the Holy Spirit you are giving me today. I ask you to guide me into truth.

In the name of Jesus Christ.

Amen."

If you have just accepted Him or you already know Him, it's now time to take His hand and allow His Spirit to direct you on your journey! Let us move forward...

9

Feelings versus Faith

As women, we must recognize that feelings and emotions are a powerful thing. They can propel the very direction of your life. Feelings create momentum, moving you upward in exhilaration, downward to depths of depression, or, many times keeping you in a holding pattern and ultimately causing tormenting confusion.

The purpose of feelings is to magnify good experiences and make us aware of negative experiences.

Yet they have a proper place and must be kept in balance according to the Word of God, otherwise they will mislead you and send you on a path of destruction.

How Are We to Live as Christian Women?

"...but the just shall live by his faith."
Habakkuk 2:4 KJV

God's Word clearly informs us that our lives are to be governed by belief, trust in Him and His unchanging Word. I understand the struggle between feelings versus choosing to believe what the written Word declares.

Below is a list of the feelings I endured. Yet with the encouragement of the Holy Spirit and the power of Jesus Christ, He caused me to overcome each one and He'll do the same for you as you accept His direction.

- Lost my joy for life (felt drained).

- Lost self-esteem and confidence.

- Isolated myself from family and friends (no longer wanted to hear their varied comments on how to "fix" the situation).

- Lost my identity—began altering my personality and appearance numerous times in an ongoing effort to please my spouse.

- Lost mental "boundaries"— began second guessing myself (could no longer determine what behaviors were right or wrong).

- Felt a "cloak of shame, guilt, and condemnation placed upon me.

- Smiled on the outside and cried on the inside.

- Lived under a mask of silence and denial – (thinking it's not that bad; if I don't talk about it or address it, the situation will get better; it's okay).

- Endured a sense of hopelessness, frustration, and depression.

- Began entertaining thoughts of suicide (feeling this situation is too painful, too shameful; I can't take it anymore).

Determine today to trust in Jesus Christ as the propeller for your life, **not** your feelings. As I gave my shattered heart to the Lord, He removed my shame so I could finally "lift up my face and head" from the inside.

> "But You, O Lord, are a shield for me, my glory, and the lifter up of my head."
> Psalms 3:3

As you continue reading, become aware of your feelings and determine if you're making judgments and decisions on feelings <u>versus</u> faith.

Yes, one cannot deny feelings, yet they must be kept within the boundaries of the Word of God so you are not deceived. I, too, had to make the choice of being led by my "feelings" or to make a decision and trust God and His Word by faith.

In trusting Him, I was able to grasp the Scriptural truth that: "if the unbelieving departs, let him depart. It is better to live in peace."

"But if the unbelieving partner [actually] leaves, let him do so; in such [cases the remaining] brother or sister is not morally bound. But God has called us to peace."
1 Corinthians 7:15

During the separation and after the divorce, my heart grieved over the death of the relationship and the death of my expectations. Yet I also experienced a greater degree of peace and rest to my soul than I had ever known before. The Lord was restoring my soul as I cried out for His comfort and His strength.

As we continue, you will discover the humbling, yet healing path the Lord placed in front of me.

Jesus Christ restored my broken heart and my broken wing... in stages and degrees, one sinew and one muscle at a time. He desires to heal you too as you decide to cooperate with His plan for your life.

10

Stop the Blame Game!

As you continue in this guidebook you will discover that the most powerful tool mankind is given at birth is FREE WILL!

God in His Sovereignty could have chosen for us to act like robots, to automatically follow through, yet He chose to give us CHOICE. He intentionally pours out His love upon you, desiring for you *to make* a choice of your own free will to enter into a love relationship with Him.

> *"Or are you [so blind as] to trifle with and presume upon and despise and underestimate the wealth of His kindness and forbearance and long-enduring patience? Are you mindful or actually ignorant [of the fact] that <u>God's kindness is intended to lead you to repent</u>—to change your mind and inner man to accept God's will?"*
> Romans 2:4

The purpose of God's kindness is to lead us towards Him and to want to change our ways to His ways.

He desires for you to freely come to Him without pressure, compulsion, or obligation. Whenever you use free will choice to go God's way, then He knows you genuinely love Him in return.

Sadly, with the power of choice, man can also decide to go *against* the life-giving way of God.

If you are separated or divorced because of an abusive marriage, consider the following points:

1. The Lord despises the separation or termination of the marriage covenant. (Malachi 2:16)

2. Yet, He loves you the one who has been offended and treated treacherously and prefers for you to be safe rather than dead! (Malachi 2:14,16)

3. He desires for the offender to repent, change his way and come back to God. (Ezekiel 18:21,30,31)

4. If you are in a season of separation, both the offended one and the offender should use the time wisely.

The Offended One – Seek direction and comfort from the Lord, begin learning about healthy boundaries in marriage and enforcing them; establish accountability for the offender; over a period of time look for measurable steps and behavioral changes in your spouse.

For more information on healthy boundaries, see the suggested reading materials in the back of this book.

The Offender – Acknowledge the error of his behavior, ask for the offended one's forgiveness, and repent (a genuine willingness to change his ways by demonstrating change in behavioral patterns). Repent means he must change his ways 180 degrees and return to God's way of doing things.

God makes us solely responsible and accountable for ourselves. Nowhere in the Scriptures will you find you are accountable for someone else! If you have been attempting to control or manipulate your spouse into changing or if you have been enabling him by allowing his inappropriate behavior to continue, you must choose to recognize the error of your ways. **We do not have the right or authority to control anyone, nor the right to be controlled by another individual!**

The laws of the universe dictate that we each will receive the fruit of our doings whether they are good or bad.

"Great in counsel and mighty in deeds; Whose eyes are open upon all the ways of the sons of men, to reward or repay to each one according to his ways and according to the fruit of his doing."
Jeremiah 32:19

When you continue to excuse or ignore inappropriate behavior, you are ultimately accepting it. You are doing an injustice to yourself, your children and to the offender when you refuse to acknowledge unhealthy behavior. As with earthly children, there are times in life when the child must learn to bear the consequences of unacceptable behavior. The same is true for your mate. You are not to control him, manipulate him, or to excuse his unacceptable behaviors. Your concerns are **best** addressed by prayer to the Lord. He alone has the **sole** authority and responsibility of changing your mate.

You always have the right to set healthy boundaries and you are the one who ultimately determines how you allow others to treat you. In a calm yet respectful tone, you have a right to say to the offending one:

"Honey, you may choose to speak and act this way at the moment, yet, I choose to respect myself, so I will leave the room until you can speak to me in a calmer, more respectful manner."

Or

"Honey, I love you as a person; **yet** your behavior towards me (name the exact inappropriate behavior) is not acceptable."

Then kindly inform your spouse of the way you prefer to be treated. This is the manner in which God relates to us! He loves us unconditionally, yet He **will not condone** sinful behaviors and attitudes.

If your mate has abandoned you because you have decided to set healthy boundaries with a desire to live a righteous life, you are not bound, nor should you allow yourself to be deceived by condemnation.

> *"And if any woman has an unbelieving husband, and he consents to live with her, she should not leave or divorce him.*
>
> *But if the unbelieving partner [actually] leaves, let him do so; in such [cases the remaining] brother or sister is not morally bound. But God has called us to peace."*
> 1 Corinthians 7:13,15

If you are divorced as a result of abuse, the Lord desires for you to be free from shame, guilt, and condemnation.

> *"He said to them, Because of the hardness (stubbornness and perversity) of your hearts Moses permitted you to dismiss and repudiate and divorce your wives; but from the beginning it has not been so [ordained]."*
> Matthew 19:8

As in my case, if you have had to divorce because of the insensitive, calloused heart of a spouse that is unwilling to change abusive behavioral patterns or who has abandoned you for taking a stand on the truth of God's Word, it is <u>not</u> the Lord's will for you to remain feeling condemned or in bondage for severing that type of relationship.

Today, ask the Lord for forgiveness, then receive (accept) His forgiveness. Allow Him to make you, fresh, brand new, and pure as snow. He promises to remember your past sins no more. He promises to separate your sin as far as possible from you (as far as the east is from the west), and He promises to throw that issue into the "sea of forgetfulness."

> *"He then goes on to say, And their sins and their lawbreakings I will remember no more."*
> Hebrews 10:17

> *"For as the heavens are high above the earth, so great are His mercy and loving-kindness toward those who reverently and worshipfully fear him.*
>
> *As far as the east is from the west, so far has He removed our transgressions from us."*
> Psalms 103:11,12

Jesus Christ desires for you to spiritually mature and change. If you cooperate with His program, His goal is to move you into the new quality of life He has predestined for you today!

11

To Whose Voice Are You Listening?

"The sheep that are My own hear and are listening to My voice, and I know them and they follow Me."
John 10:27

In this section you'll discover that at any moment in time you have many voices vying for attention in your head and lobbying for your choice. Your head is swirling with thoughts yet there is only one voice that truly matters and will never lead you astray. The voice of the Lord! By the Holy Spirit, He will gently guide you into truth and back on course!

I finally had a "wake up" call! I had allowed poor choices and behavior to continue and it was stealing my health physically, mentally and emotionally. I would come home from work, change my clothes and go straight to bed just to cry myself to sleep, expecting to hear from my husband the next day.

One March day I realized I'd had enough of poor choices and now I desperately desired to seek the Lord and choose His way to get my footing back onto solid ground.

God says when we choose His way we will find vital energy (during my ordeal I'd lost it). When I chose His way, I could confidently know it was already tried, tested, and proven and would protect me.

I FINALLY became ready to find my way out of the maze of confusion, by following HIS way—the way that was not a dead end and would lead me back to life.

"As for God, His way is perfect! The Word of the Lord is tested and tried; He is a shield to all those who take refuge and put their trust in Him."
Psalms 18:30

There are many voices in the world vying for YOUR attention (your choice). Let's look at these voices in detail. You have a choice to listen to the voice of the Lord and His Word or to go your own way: that includes opinions, family traditions, and old thinking patterns.

YOU CAST THE DECIDING VOTE!

Who Are the Voices?

The voices come from the Lord (God Almighty and His Son, Jesus Christ), the Devil, others and you.

As we look at the voices in detail, we must cover historical ground to ensure a common understanding.

There are opposing spiritual forces in this world: **God Almighty and His Son, Jesus Christ** versus the **devil** (satan, fallen angel, Lucifer; "god of this world"). Each operates the power of CHOICE yet with different outcomes.

A) **God Almighty** – The Sovereign Creator and Ruler of the Universe. God CHOSE you before you even knew Him! Whenever God speaks, His sole desire is to direct you towards the way of life! See 2 Thessalonians 2:13; Psalms 33:12; Deuteronomy 7:6-9

B) **Jesus Christ** – He was sent to earth by God so you may have life and enjoy it to the fullest extent! Christ came to expose and overcome satan (his strategies and damaging effects) from destroying your life.

> "...I came that they may have and enjoy life, and have it in abundance—to the full, till it overflows."
> John 10:10

> "...The reason the Son of God was made manifest (visible) was to undo (destroy, loosen, and dissolve) the works the devil [has done]."
> I John 3:8b

By choosing to lay down His life for you, He also made the following rights available to you:

1. He redeemed you (bought you back) from the curses of the Law, satan, and all its effects. (See the curses of the Law recorded in Deuteronomy chapter 28).

> *"Christ purchased our freedom (redeeming us) from the curse (doom) of the Law's (condemnation), by [Himself] becoming a curse for us, for it is written [in the Scriptures], Cursed is everyone who hangs on a tree (is crucified)."*
> Galatians 3:13

2. Jesus Christ can heal your broken heart, open your (spiritually-blinded) eyes to the truth about your life and set you free from bondages placed upon you by satan.

> *"The Spirit of the Lord is upon me, because the Lord has anointed and qualified me to preach the Gospel of good tidings to the meek, the poor and afflicted; He has sent me to bind up and heal the brokenhearted, to proclaim liberty to the [physical and spiritual] captives, and the opening of the prison and of the eyes to those who are bound."*
> Isaiah 61:1

3. Jesus Christ exchanged or took your sin so you may have His righteousness. We'll discover more of this truth in Section 2 under Freedom Key 4. (Ephesians 2:4-10)

4. Jesus Christ tore down the wall separating you from God. His shed blood enables you to have a personal relationship with God instead of a shallow religious experience. You can now come freely before God and pour out your heart and He hears you.

> *"But now in Christ Jesus, you who once were [so] far away, through (by, in) the blood of Christ have been brought near.*
>
> *For He is [Himself] our peace—our bond of unity and harmony. He has made us both [Jew and Gentile] one (body), and has broken down (destroyed, abolished) the hostile dividing wall between us."*
> Ephesians 2:13,14

47

C) **Satan**[1] – Formerly named Lucifer (Isaiah 14:12), one of the three archangels created by God. He wrongfully chose to rebel against God, consequently God cast him out of heaven and eternally cursed him as satan (the adversary) (Ezekiel 28:13-19; Isaiah 14:12-15; Revelation 12:17). When he speaks, his sole mission is to steal, to kill, and to destroy the quality of your life! His name means "adversary." He masks his words, making them sound logical and outright reasonable, yet in the **end** his way always brings disappointment. He is called the "deceiver, father of lies, accuser, and a thief." His plan is to pervert and distort God's plan for your life, your family and to discredit the Word of truth.

> *"The thief comes only in order that he may steal and may kill and may destroy..."*
> John 10:10

Mankind's corruption under satan came about as a direct result of Adam's choice to disobey God in the Garden of Eden. The consequences and corresponding curses of disobedience detailed in Deuteronomy 28 were passed on to **all** of mankind's successive generations.

The truth is that satan did NOT deceive Adam, he was fully aware of his actions and the corresponding consequences of his poor choice. Adam's disobedient action brought sin and all of its damaging effects upon everyone who is born into this world!

> *"And it was not Adam who was deceived, but [the] woman who was deceived and deluded and fell into transgression."*
> 1 Timothy 2:14

> *"Therefore as sin came into the world through one man and death as the result of sin, so death spread to all men [no one being able to stop it or escape its power] because all men sinned."*
> Romans 5:12

As recorded in the Parable of the Sower and the Seed, satan's plan is to steal the Word of God from taking root in your heart and actions (your life). He uses the cares of this world, distractions, criticisms from others, riches, pleasures to take your eyes off what the Lord is directing you to fulfill.

He wants to rob the joy from your life and to ultimately take your life.

"Listen then to the parable of the sower and the seed.

While anyone is hearing the Word of the kingdom and does not grasp and comprehend it, the evil one comes and snatches away what is sown in the heart. This is what was sown along the roadside.

As for what was sown on thin (rocky) soil, this is he who hears the Word and at once welcomes and accepts it with joy;

Yet it has no real root in himself, but is temporary— inconstant, lasts but a little while and when affliction or trouble or persecution comes on account of the Word, at once he is caused to stumble—he is repelled and begins to distrust and desert Him Whom he ought to trust and obey, and he falls away.

As for what was sown among the thorns, this is he who hears the Word, but the cares of the world and the pleasure and delight and glamour and deceitfulness of riches choke and suffocate the Word, and it yields no fruit.

As for what was sown on good soil, this is he who hears the Word and grasps and comprehends it; he indeed bears fruit, and yields in one case a hundred times as much as was sown, in another sixty times as much, and in another thirty."
Matthew 13:18-23

Satan, "the accuser of the brethren," sets up circumstances in your childhood and/or adult life to destroy you *or* the quality of your remaining existence here on earth. He then turns around and blames you for the chaos which **he** brought upon your life! Unknowingly, you then take upon yourself the weight of satan's inflicted shame, guilt, self-hatred, or condemnation!

Satan, the "god" of HOPELESSNESS only speaks lies **about** you and **to** you regarding your life.

God and His Word operate on CAUSE and EFFECT. Choose HIS way and you will enter into the way of life, blessing and peace. He has promised His Words cannot be broken and will not fall void to the ground. Whenever His Words are used, dynamic power is released into your life!

When you choose to hear and act upon the voices **other** than God's written or revealed Word, you have chosen to position yourself for a fall and ultimately **great** disappointment.

12

Testing Your Choices

"There is a way which seems right to a man and appears straight before him, but at the end of it are the ways of death."
Proverbs 14:12

From all outward indications, your way may appear "right." Yet unless it aligns with God's perspective, you are destined to run into a dead-end road. Let's look at the elements of a poor choice versus a quality choice.

Poor choices are caused by:

1. Ignorance–not having the RIGHT instruction or information on a matter.

2. Willful Disobedience–possessing the right information or instruction **YET** willfully deciding to go the other direction.

3. Fear–afraid of or lack of trust in following God's instruction.

Quality choices are caused by:

1. Instruction–recognizing Godly direction as written in the Word of God.

2. Obedience–acting upon, and applying the instruction revealed in the Word of God.

3. Faith–trusting that God's direction is always for YOU and your children's benefit (for the immediate and long term).

Unfortunately most people make decisions out of FEAR and "GOING BY FEELINGS" instead of a position of FAITH and TRUST in God's promises!

TIP! Regarding choices–God will always be the FIRST one to talk to you about your life. If you don't listen He will send another, a "human messenger" to confirm what He has already instructed you to do. If you continue without heeding His way, He will graciously step aside and let you learn the "fruit" of YOUR way. He does this so we can grow up and LEARN to walk the way of truth.

> *"I, the Lord, search the mind, I try the heart, even to give*
> *every man according to his ways, according to the fruit of his*
> *doings."*
> Jeremiah 17:10

Finally with just weeks before the divorce date, a portion of my initial shock, bewilderment, and disappointment about the broken relationship wore off. I had to honestly ask, "Lord, how did I get to this low point?" After much prayer and soul searching He began revealing the following to me...

On the day we take our first breath we are each equipped with an EMPOWERMENT, the ability of choice by free will. The dictionary describes choice as **"the act of selection, the power or right to choose."**

As children, you may have been taught HOW to exercise choice by free will depending upon how your parents or caregivers raised you.

Example: "Would you prefer chicken or steak for dinner?"

If you were like most of us, your parents or caregivers made the choice(s) for you. Sometimes they chose for you up until the time you left home. As a result, especially for women, the outcome is a "withered, inactive, atrophied muscle of choice by free will."

In the cases of incest, verbal, emotional, psychological or child abuse, some of you were severely violated and even robbed of the power of choice by adults who wrongly inflicted THEIR poor choice upon you.

Out of the Maze/State of Confusion...Which Way Leads Me Out?

Apparently, my spouse had made his choice, now I had to trust the Lord to lead me into His direction for my life.

My heart was tired. It was worn down from crying and being confused about my crumbling marriage. At this point I was going through a third separation within one year. I wanted a "passport" out of my "state of confusion." My heart became shredded like meat in a butcher's grinder from the numerous separations and ached from relying upon countless broken promises. I could no longer continue to exist by hanging in a dazed, ineffective state of limbo.

In March 1999 at six in the morning, my heart was directed to this verse:

> *"**Arise** [From the depression and prostration in which circumstances have kept you; rise to a new life]! Shine—be radiant with the glory of the Lord; for your light is come, and the glory of the Lord is risen upon you!"*
> Isaiah 60:1

My heart finally said "enough with the crying, the pleading, and back and forth between being together then being separated. It is time to finally make a quality choice…"

> *"I call Heaven and Earth to witness this day against you, that I have set before you life and death, the blessing and the curse; therefore choose life, that you and your descendants may live;*
>
> *To love the Lord your God, to obey His voice, and to cling to Him; for He is your life, and the length of your days…"*
> Deuteronomy 30:19,20

Let's look at the fork in the road of CHOICE…

Way of Life (God's Way)	Way of Death (Satan's/Other's Way)
○ Mutual Marital Care/Respect	○ Dishonor/Control
○ Open Communication	○ Closed/No Communication
○ Encouragement	○ Discouragement
○ Mercy	○ Judgment
○ Honesty/Integrity	○ Deception
○ Peace	○ Confusion
○ Righteousness	○ Shame/Guilt
○ Joy	○ Discontent
○ Safety/Confidence	○ Fear/Anxiety
○ Sufficiency/Abundance	○ Lack of Provision
○ Sound Mind	○ Double Minded
○ Hope…Clean Start Each Day	○ Hopelessness… Depression/Suicide

Beware of the Valley of Indecision

Straddling in between "two opinions" will torment your mind and make you unstable. Satan enjoys keeping you in the "valley of indecision"…Yet God has an answer for you.

> *"Elijah came near to all the people, and said, 'How long will you halt and limp between two opinions? If the Lord is God, follow Him! But if Baal, then follow him.' And the people did not answer him a word."*
> I Kings 18:21

Today, God asks you the same question: **how long will you waiver between two opinions?**

Adam's sin, and its devastating effects on the family have passed from generation to generation and will continue into the NEXT generation

54

until someone takes a rightful stand believing the Word of God and the overcoming power of the Blood of Jesus Christ!

If the Holy Spirit tells you to remain, then remain, just trust and know the Lord is working out His plan for your life. He will give you the grace, wisdom, strength, and peace to endure the process.

If the Holy Spirit tells you to leave, then leave! Trust and know that He will safely lead you forward in life. Remember, the Holy Spirit is your expert tour guide, He knows what lies ahead and His plan is to get you safely through to the other side!

As recorded in the Old Testament, the Israelites experienced the "valley of decision" between their bondage and the Promised Land. The same decision point exists for you today!

Let's look at what occurs in that "valley." What exactly do we go through?

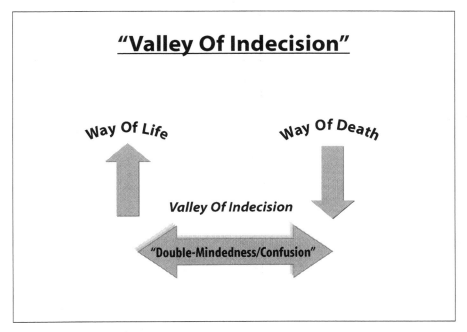

After our fourth separation and many months of crying and pleading, it became clear to me that my husband did not desire reconciliation. I could no longer remain in this "valley of indecision." I was slowly dying inside with each interaction. I had to make a quality choice to trust the prompting of the Lord. The upcoming Freedom Keys revealed truth to me during the separation, divorce, and recovery of my heart and life.

During the restoration phase, I felt as if my whole world was turned "upside down," yet in hindsight, I see the Lord's Hand actually was turning it "rightside up!" In the midst of this emotional healing, I was prompted to "let go of the past" so He could move me forward. He guided me through selling the home, scaling down by giving away furniture, and sleeping on an air mattress for two months. Within six months, He restored my finances and helped me acquire new furniture...all without debt! The Lord sustained me for several months through each step. I personally experienced "spiritual intensive care" from the Lord. His loving care included vast amounts of quiet time and personal attention from Him as He rebuilt my shattered heart and soul one piece at a time by the truths in His Word.

Today, the shameful, angry, and bitter thoughts are gone. My heart genuinely desires the richest of God's will for all parties involved! Jesus Christ alone healed my heart and soul, making them both brand new!

Only you can determine to follow the Lord's road map out of your tangled situation. He is not a "respecter" of individuals, what He does for one He can also do for you (Acts 10:34). He'll safely lead you step-by-step on your journey!

Prescription

1. You can have comfort knowing God inspired and gave us the Bible. It is beneficial for teaching you how to live life, showing you when life is awry, and finally showing you how to get back on track in life. **2 Timothy 3:16,17**

2. God desires to lead you through the "highs and lows" of your life journey. **Exodus 13:21,22; Proverbs 6:22,23**

3. You can cry out to the Lord and He will be there to safely guide your way and keep you from harm. **Psalms 5:8; Psalms 31:3,4; Psalms 61:2,3; Psalms 143:10,11**

Keys
To
Freedom

13

Key 1: Who Really Loves You?

Do you realize there is Someone who loves you unconditionally, purely, without strings attached or without any ulterior motives? Do you know this individual excitedly awaited your arrival to this earth?

> *"Before I formed you in the womb I knew and approved of you [as My chosen instrument], and before you were born I separated and set you apart, consecrating you, and I appointed you a prophet to the nations."*
> Jeremiah 1:5

God knew you from within your mother's womb. He kept a watchful eye on you. He knows every fiber of your being, and yes, He still loves you. He has mapped out a good plan for your life (Romans 8:28,29).

> *"And the rib or part of his side which the Lord God had taken from the man, He built up and made into a woman and brought her to the man."*
> Genesis 2:22

"Built up" is the Hebrew word "BANAH"[1] meaning sculpted, built up, to build. God intentionally took time designing, forming, and sculpting the female creature. You are not an afterthought! He invested time and care in your structural design.

A genuine revelation of God's love will fill in the cracks of your broken heart, strengthen a weak or failing heart, and transform a shattered heart into newness. When your heart is broken, you're unable to withstand the slightest of daily stresses! You can burst out crying while searching for lost car keys, angrily respond to cleaning up a simple spill, or isolate yourself from others in denial of your pain.

Yet, God's plan is for you to <u>enjoy your life</u> to the fullest!

59

The Bible is mankind's **"Owner's Manual for Life."** God, as the Owner of His people provides instruction on how to relate with Him, to yourself and with others.

> *"Do you not know that your body is the temple—the very sanctuary—of the Holy Spirit Who lives within you, Whom you have received [as a Gift] from God? <u>You are not your own,</u>*
>
> *<u>You were bought with a price—purchased with a preciousness and paid for, made His own.</u> So then, honor God and bring glory to Him in your body."*
> I Corinthians 6:19,20

As the "Owner's Manual," the Bible defines how God designed the optimal operating conditions for your life. It tells us the Owner's (God's) standard for living and shows when we are operating "outside of the Owner's" original guidelines. Similar to a manufacturer's operating manual, you can expect peak performance when you operate <u>according to the instructions</u>. When you choose to operate the item outside of the originally intended purpose you will experience faulty use and your improper use also "voids" the manufacturer's warranty!

The same principle is applied to God and His Word—the Bible! You must choose to operate according to His original design as outlined in the Scriptures, otherwise if you knowingly **or** unknowingly choose to operate outside of His plan **you too** will experience "faulty" life operation. God's intended blessings for you at that time will be "voided."

The Bible's sole design is an instruction guide on relationships. **Yes, I said relationships, NOT religion!**

In the Word of God, you will discover the depth of the following relationships:

1. <u>You and God</u> – Uncover the plan that He has for your life with the priceless worth and value that God places on it because of the precious blood Jesus Christ shed for you on the cross! Over time you will grasp the depth of love He specifically holds for you. There is no hole too deep from which the Lord's arm cannot pull you up and out of when you call upon Him.

"Surely the arm of the Lord is not too short to save, nor his ear too dull to hear."
Isaiah 59:1 NIV

"Let your character or moral disposition be free from love of money—[including] greed, avarice, lust, and craving for earthly possessions—and be satisfied with your present [circumstances and with what you have]; for He (God) Himself has said, 'I will not in any way fail you nor give you up nor leave you without support. [I will] not, [I will] not, [I will] not in any degree leave you helpless, nor forsake nor let [you] down, [relax My hold on you].—Assuredly not!'"
Hebrews 13:5

Isn't that a comforting and empowering truth to reflect upon?

His grace and mercy are so overflowing that when you sin, err or "blow it," God made a way for the shame and guilt to wash off of you by directly going to Him!

"If we [freely] admit that we have sinned and confess our sins, He is faithful and just [true to His own nature and promises] and will forgive our sins (dismiss our lawlessness) and <u>continuously cleanse</u> us from all unrighteousness— everything not in conformity to His will in purpose, thought and action."
I John 1:9

God did not design your mind and heart to be weighed down with the burden of condemnation. You will learn more about this truth in Chapter 17.

2. <u>Your Relationship with Yourself</u> – The "Owners Manual" defines your uniqueness, your true identity, and the true worth God places upon your life because of the PRICELESS shed blood of Christ. It shows you how to love and respect yourself in a balanced manner. Do you realize He gave each

one of us distinctive traits so we could stand apart as a "one of a kind" masterpiece?

Each of us received a unique DNA code, fingerprints, retina patterns, a distinct appearance, skin coloring, and so on. God intentionally designed you as "Special Edition #1!"

3. <u>Your Relationships with Others</u> –The "Owner's Manual" clearly defines healthy God-given boundaries in relationships and the consequences of unhealthy boundaries. It defines the God-given boundaries in relating as spouses, parents with younger children, adult children, others in the Body Of Christ, co-workers, business associates, and neighbors.

> *"For the Word that God speaks is alive and full of power [making it active, operative, energizing, and effective]; it is sharper than any two-edged sword, penetrating to the dividing line of the breath of life (soul) and [the immortal] spirit, and of joints and marrow [of the deepest parts of our nature], <u>exposing and sifting and analyzing and judging the very thoughts and purposes of the heart.</u>*
>
> *And not a creature exists that is concealed from His sight, but all things are open and exposed, naked and defenseless to the eyes of Him with Whom we have to do."*
> Hebrews 4:12,13

> *"God means what he says. What he says goes. His powerful Word is sharp as a surgeon's scalpel, <u>cutting through everything</u>, whether doubt or defense, laying us open to listen and obey.*
>
> *Nothing and no one is impervious to God's Word. We can't get away from it—no matter what."*
> Hebrews 4:12,13 MSG

God's Word will tell you <u>what</u> is right, which is a greater value than <u>who</u> is right!

The Owner's Manual will help you identify the unhealthy personal motives, purposes and heart schemes that determined your former choice patterns. As you first learn, then begin applying God's Word <u>you will shift</u> to the path of using healthier communication and relationship behaviors.

Upon spending time in the Bible, you'll realize it's the, *most endearing love story* you'll ever read. It's about a God who pursues His people one-by-one with an all-consuming love so they may come to know Him. When you really grasp the depth of God's love, you will make a choice to run to Him, **not** away from Him and you will begin desiring only His plan for your life.

Today, decide to bring all of the broken pieces of your heart to Him, ask Him to heal it fully and make it new, so He can use your life again.

> *"The Lord is close to those who are of a broken heart, and*
> *saves such as are crushed with sorrow for sin and are*
> *humbly and thoroughly penitent."*
> Psalms 34:18

God wants you to realize He loved you unconditionally before you knew Him. He desires a personal and intimate relationship with you starting today! He has good plans for you and can turn things around when you trust Him.

Quality Choice:

You must learn to care <u>more</u> about God's unconditional love and acceptance of you rather than people's opinions or approval.

Prescription 1

1. God took His time in designing and sculpting you. You are NOT an afterthought; you are a distinctly made creation. **Genesis 2:22**

2. God knew you before you were born and watched you being formed in the womb. He knows every intimate detail of your life, and loves you unconditionally. **Psalms 139:1-7, 13-18**

3. God cannot forget you, and He has tattooed an image of you on the palm of His hand to ensure your face is always in His clear view. **Isaiah 49:15,16**

4. God will never forsake you. Even if your natural parents have turned away from you, God promises to adopt you as His very own. **Psalm 27:10**

5. God unconditionally chose to extend His love to you, while you were a sinner and even before you knew Him. He sent His Son to die for you and cleanse you so you could have a personal and intimate relationship with Him. God has a burning desire for you to grasp the depth of His love for you and His care for every aspect of your life. **I John 4:9, 10; Romans 5:8,9; John 3:16,17; Ephesians 3:15-19**

6. Genuine love means a corresponding action. God so loved that He GAVE His Son to show that commitment. Love is not a "gushy" feeling. Genuine unconditional love equals a corresponding obedient action. When we choose to obey God, His Word and His way then we are showing our love for Him. **I John 5:3**

7. Begin referring to <u>My Daily Confessions</u> listed in chapter 25 of this guidebook. Start speaking these truths aloud to begin discovering God's perspective on your life. Review truths 1-15.

Practical Exercises

✔ Three times a day (morning, midday, bedtime) for the next 21 days: Stop, look directly into your eyes in a mirror and say, *"I have been bought with a price, I do not belong to myself, God loves me, so I love myself too!"*

✔ Hug yourself while repeating this declaration.

✔ Each time you have an unpleasant thought about yourself or you receive an unkind comment from others, REMIND or repeat to yourself *"God loves me, so I love myself."*

✔ Learn to claim **I John 1:9**—acknowledge your sins, errors of your ways, **and** RECEIVE (accept) God's forgiveness.

Begin recording instances of learning to accept God's forgiveness in a journal.

14

Key 2: Are You a Builder or a Buster? The Power of Words

***

"Death and life are in the power of the tongue, and they who indulge it shall eat the fruit of it [for death or life]."
Proverbs 18:21

Do you know or realize that words possess inherent power! Words have the ability to heal, to build up, or to tear down and even destroy. Words are motivated from one of two sources: from God and His Word or from satan.

Moving forward from an abusive marriage, I had to make a choice to trust God and His Words about rebuilding my heart, soul, and mind <u>or</u> to mistakenly listen to satan's chaotic and destructive words.

As the earlier Scripture stated, we each live by the "fruit" of our mouth, whether it is good or rotten. Our words BECOME our thoughts, which in turn become our ACTIONS.

Since I so desperately wanted my heart, soul, and mind to heal, I had to daily and sometimes moment-by-moment deliberately filter and make a conscious choice of the type of words which I spoke about myself, to myself, and toward others in my life.

Our God is a God of hope! The power of His spoken Word brought light into a dark and chaotic situation when He formed the heavens and the earth. He constructed an orderly universe with His Words.

You too choose the quality of your construction materials—do you want to build up or tear down in your life?

What dark, disorderly situation do you need to bring into orderly light? If you're seriously ready to begin "redesigning" your life, learn to speak TO and ABOUT yourself, <u>and</u> the situation using God's Words!

"So any person who knows what is right to do but <u>does not do</u> it, to him it is sin."
James 4:17

Start changing your life by choosing to SPEAK words of LIFE! Initially you will meet people who are "naysayers," and even your own negative words will occasionally pop up. Yet, like the Apostle Paul as recorded in Acts 28:3-6, when satan (the serpent, the accuser of the brethren, the father of lies) comes to you with words CONTRARY to God (poison), you must learn to "shake it off" and move forward with the Lord!

Start today, with ONE encouraging truth from God's Word about yourself… one word at a time. You can start by saying "I am priceless to Jesus Christ because He poured out His precious blood for me!"

"Do two walk together, except they make an appointment and <u>have agreed</u>?"
Amos 3:3

To walk with God, you must make a choice to line up your words with how He speaks about you and your life. You must be in agreement with Him.

It doesn't matter what other people say about you, yet it does matter what you say to yourself! Your life will change when you begin to align your words with God's vocabulary about yourself.

Jesus Christ poured out His precious, priceless blood for you on Calvary so that you may be set free from satan's lies and bondage.

Jesus Christ is in your corner, supporting you on this healing journey. He will not let you down and, if you do fall, He wants you to get back up, then quickly and boldly run to Him for assistance.

"Let us then fearlessly and confidently and boldly draw near to the throne of grace—the throne of God's unmerited favor [to us sinners]; that we may receive mercy [for our failures] and find grace to help in good time for every need—appropriate help and well-timed help, coming just when we need it."
Hebrews 4:16

Jesus Christ will see that you are VICTORIOUS!

Let us see how words can impact your thoughts and ultimately your daily choices. If I say the word "ice cream," what comes into your mind? If I say it often enough some of you are already designing rich sundaes in your mind. Other people may want to head towards the refrigerator right now to get some ice cream. What prompted the behavioral response? One word…"ice cream."

This chart shows how the progression of words impacts your daily behavior.

Building Blocks Of Words

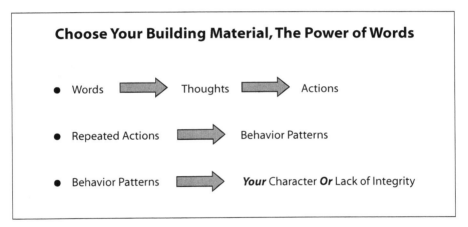

Choose Your Building Material, The Power of Words

- Words ➡ Thoughts ➡ Actions

- Repeated Actions ➡ Behavior Patterns

- Behavior Patterns ➡ *Your* Character *Or* Lack of Integrity

Challenge yourself today to begin thinking about the WORDS you speak about yourself, your life, and about others. (Why not change them today to match the way God speaks of you?)

Quality Choice:

God gave you FREE WILL. Choose today which type of words you will hold in your mind, about yourself, and over the lives of others…choose words of LIFE!

Prescription 2

1. God has elevated His Word above His own name. He sent us His Word to heal you and deliver you from destruction. His Word shows us how to live; it is "rock solid" and cannot be broken (whether or not you choose to believe it). **Psalms 138:2; Psalms 107:20; Isaiah 45:22,23; Matthew 4:4**

2. The power of God's Words gave birth and formation to the heavens and the earth.**Genesis 1:3,6,11,14, 20,24,26,28,29; Psalms 90:2**

3. Words have the ability to produce good or rotten fruit. When you choose to speak and act upon God's Words you will have life and "light" in the situation. **Proverbs 4:4; Proverbs 18:21**

4. The Word of God will bring healing, life, sweetness, and soundness into your life. **Proverbs 15:26; 16:24; 12:18; 12:25; 15:4**

5. You can choose to line up your words with God's Words about yourself. Determine today, to begin speaking about yourself from God's perspective. Choose to "change your tune" and allow Him to put a "new song" in your mouth, one of praise and thankfulness. **Psalms 91; Psalms 100:4; Psalms 119:164; Amos 3:3; Ephesians 4:29-31; Hebrews 13:15**

6. Continue reading Chapter 25 <u>My Daily Confessions</u> statements 16-30 to discover the words God declares about you!

Practical Exercises

✔ Explain the effect of positive and negative words in your mind. (Proverbs 18:21)

✔ How did Jesus Christ say you are to live? (Matthew 4:4)

✔ How does the tongue impact your life? (James 3:5-13)

✔ Why are you to do <u>all</u> things without murmuring, grumbling, faultfinding and complaining? (Philippians 2:14,15)

✔ When does murmuring, grumbling, faultfinding, and complaining usually occur in a person's life? (Philippians 4:6)

✔ What are you to do <u>instead</u> of murmuring, grumbling, faultfinding, and complaining? (Philippians 4:6)

15

Key 3: Food for Thought— Woman, What Are You Thinking?

As we discovered in the previous chapter, words are containers of **power**, loaded with the dynamic ability to build up or to tear down.

Can you recall instances in your life when words accomplished a negative effect? Now recall when words accomplished a positive effect in your life. Just take a moment to reflect, now consider the contrasting outcomes of <u>each</u> effect in your life.

Words placed together become *thoughts*, and it is the power of thoughts that conduct the "train" of your life. On what track is your locomotive running? Thoughts can take you upward, closer to God and into His presence for guidance, comfort, and restoration. Thoughts can also take the downward track, spiraling you into satan's camp with ideas of despair, depression, hopelessness, and even death (suicidal thoughts).

I know this personally because I have ridden on both tracks. Yet the Lord in His infinite mercy and grace intervened at the station of depression and asked me to make a choice. I recall the morning after many tears and prayers, while reading the Scriptures, the Holy Spirit spoke to me: "Michele, arise and get up from that negative mindset in which circumstances have placed you and make the choice to follow me or to follow the road to death (Isaiah 60:1). <u>You</u> must be the one to make the choice!"

Those words snapped me out of it! With tears still in my eyes, I sat up and boldly cried out loud, "Yes, Lord help me. I choose life!"

I got out of bed, showered, changed my tear-stained bed linen and jumped into the day with a fresh vigor for the next steps that the Lord had planned for me. From that day, He started the gentle "U-turn" of my life by lovingly guiding me back to the path of light.

Woman...What Are You Thinking?

Have you ever stopped to think about what you're thinking about???

The human mind is like a VHS tape, constantly recording your life moments. It vividly captures each experience. How far back in time can you recall?

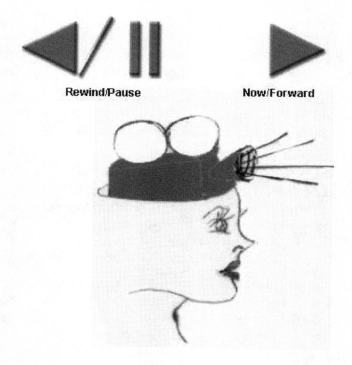

Rewind/Pause   Now/Forward

While in the healing phase after the divorce, when I heard certain words or drove by certain places, the "video recorder" of my mind would quickly flash back to a particular moment in time. Usually the thought connection would bring me to tears or even flashing anger!

I cried out to the Lord to help me and to please make the "pain" go away. During the prayer, He gave me the image of a VCR in my mind.

The thoughts you meditate upon actually project an image in your mind. Thoughts of the **past** bring only regret, shame, condemnation, oppression, and depression. The Lord wanted to move me *FORWARD*, yet I was allowing my mind to drift, linger and sometimes "camp out" for days in the past! I realized that until I let go of the thoughts of the past, the Lord was unable to move my life forward! **By constantly pressing the "rewind or pause" button of my mind, I unknowingly was sabotaging God's plan of progression for my life.**

From the Scriptures, it became clear God wanted to move me forward, yet I was allowing myself and the suggestions of satan to keep me in a tormented "holding" pattern. Here's a truth to consider...you can only move in one direction at a time!

The same God who spoke with Isaiah, challenged me to trust Him with my future, by sharing the same message with me:

> *"Forget about what's happened; don't keep going over old history.*
>
> *Be alert; be present. I'm about to do something brand new. It's bursting out! Don't you see it? There it is! I'm making a road through the desert, rivers in the badlands.*
> Isaiah 43:18,19 MSG

The same God that spoke with the Apostle Paul shared with me..." Michele, you need to live in the NOW...stop looking in the past, *enjoy NOW and TRUST Me with your future*! Now are you ready to move on?"

> *"Friends, don't get me wrong: By no means do I count myself an expert in all of this, but I've got my eye on the goal, where God is beckoning us onward—to Jesus. I'm off and running, and I'm not turning back."*
> Philippians 3:13 MSG

You are the only one who can decide if you want to move forward or remain in a holding pattern by allowing your mind to "stockpile old VHS tapes" or by re-pressing the rewind/pause button in your mind.

Today, I can look to my past as a point of learning and growth, no longer a source of pain. My "now" and "future" hopes are so exciting, that I daily thank the Lord for teaching me this truth!

As you continue in this chapter, you will learn more on how your thoughts **DO** determine your response to life.

What are **your** thoughts? The Bible teaches you how to properly think in this life about yourself.

Do you realize that your daily thoughts <u>impact</u> the direction and quality of your life?

> *"For as he thinks in his heart, so is he."*
> Proverbs 23:7

This guidebook is a book about making quality choices. Your thoughts and belief systems determine your life outcome. If you want to change your life then you must begin to change your thinking patterns!

The Bible records that there are only two ways of thinking: one is right thinking, the other is wrong thinking. I don't mean to simplify things, yet God in His infinite wisdom made it clear for us to see the existence of two paths in life.

Let's first look at Wrong Thinking:

Wrong thinking occurs whenever you contradict the way of God's Word, His thoughts and His direction. Your limited thinking will always cause you to miss the target and fall short of His victory prize for your life.

Examples of Wrong Thinking

Genesis 18:9-15; Genesis 21:1-7

Sarah – She laughed at God because she trusted more in her aging anatomy than the promise that God spoke to her. She wrongly thought that her physical limitations were greater than God's ability to fulfill His promise! God corrected her wrong thinking by directly confronting her. He fulfilled the promise He had spoken and at ninety years of age, Sarah gave birth to the promised male child.

What physical or other "limitations" are you using as an excuse in your life? Today God challenges you to see through His <u>unlimited</u> perspective for your life!

II Samuel 9:1-3, II Samuel 4:4-6

Mephibosheth – He was born the child of a King, rightful heir to a throne, yet had a shameful, beggar mentality and inferiority complex because he grew up lame in both feet. He wrongly thought he was unworthy to sit at the king's table.

If you hold a "Mephibosheth mindset," today the Holy Spirit boldly declares to you: **"You are _NOT_ unworthy! You <u>are worthy</u> because of the value Jesus Christ places upon your life. So stop groveling and settling for crumbs under the table. Come out from under the table and sit up here in <u>your rightful place</u> next to Christ, the King! Get up today! Arise!"**

Examples Of Right Thinking

I Samuel 17:28-47

Young David – He confidently knew his true identity through the eyes of the Living God and not through his family's lowly perception of him. He triumphantly overcame the giant Goliath because David trusted God's perspective of the situation.

Daniel 6:3-14, 19-23

Daniel – He knew his true identity so he was not shaken when others attempted to discredit him to his employer or colleagues. Daniel overcame the accusations of others because he trusted God's perspective through the matter.

God solely designed your mind to meditate upon, feed upon, live upon, and to be guided by His Word.

God calls thinking contrary to His, "evil." This truth is shown in the story of the twelve spies who went to survey the Promised Land. Only two men thought and spoke of the situation as God had declared. The ten others became afraid and refuted God. He called that an "evil report" and it displeased Him. See Numbers 13:1-3; 26-33; 14:26-38. Whenever you choose not to believe God, you place yourself in a displeasing position before him.

What are your strongholds?

A stronghold is a destructive pattern of thoughts built up or developed in your mind. It is a fortress, a series of lies or deceptions embedded, literally grooved as a thought pattern which drives your mind's decision process.

These strongholds develop in your head during your childhood or you have placed them there in response to a situation you experienced later in life. They become your way of thinking about and responding to a situation.

A stronghold literally runs your life. It becomes your "security" wall and determines how you make decisions.

How do you break your stronghold?

By taking EACH thought and bringing it captive in submission to Jesus Christ's Words.

> *"For the weapons of our warfare are not physical (weapons of flesh and blood), but they are mighty before God for the overthrow and destruction of strongholds.*
>
> *[Inasmuch as we] refute arguments and theories and reasonings and every proud and lofty thing that sets itself up against the (true) knowledge of God; and <u>we lead every thought and purpose away captive into the obedience of Christ, the Messiah, the Anointed One.</u>"*
> II Corinthians 10:4,5

The power of choice gives you an awesome freedom, but also carries with it an awesome responsibility! It is up to you day-by-day, or in some cases, moment-by-moment to exercise the RIGHT choice in your thoughts to get the desired outcome.

Yes, you can actually <u>train your mind</u> to deliberately choose what you think! One thought at a time.

Do you realize that, where your mind GOES, your actions follow?

78

Left in its unchecked, natural state, the human mind runs wild like a young puppy. It runs carelessly loose and without purpose until it is brought into the owner's subjection with a collar or leash.

Let us discover <u>how to retrain</u> the mind and <u>how to break</u> the cycle of your destructive thinking patterns.

How to Break Your Destructive Cycle

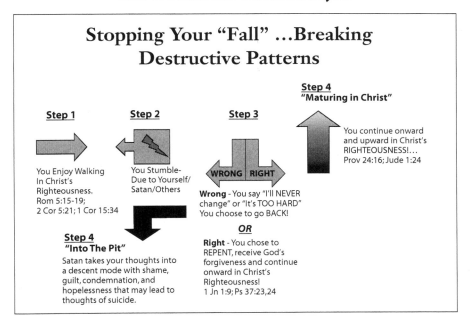

1) **Realize God made you Righteous** – You accept a relationship with God through His Son, Jesus Christ (Romans 10:9,10). At that moment, God has given you His **free gift** of righteousness. He also releases you (acquits you) from sin. Due to Christ's accomplishment God now enables <u>you</u> to come before His presence <u>without</u> any sense of shame, guilt, condemnation or inferiority. God now sees <u>you</u> as sinless and in "right standing or right relationship" with Him!

*"But God's **free gift** is not at all to be compared to the trespass—His grace is out of all proportion to the fall of man. For if many died through one man's falling away—his lapse, his offense—much more profusely did God's grace and the **free gift** [that comes] through the undeserved favor of the one Man Jesus Christ, abound and overflow to and for [the benefit of] many.*

*Nor is the **free gift** at all to be compared to the effect of that one [man's] sin. For the sentence [following the trespass] of one [man] brought condemnation, whereas the **free gift** [following] many transgressions brings justification—an act of righteousness.*

*For if, because of one man's trespass [lapse, offense] death reigned through that one, much more surely will those who receive [God's] overflowing grace (unmerited favor) and the **free gift of righteousness** <u>(putting them into right standing with Himself)</u> reign as kings in life through the One, Jesus Christ the Messiah, the Anointed One.*

Well then, as one man's trespass—one man's false step and falling away—[led] to condemnation for all men, so <u>one Man's act of righteousness [leads] to acquittal and right standing with God,</u> and life for all men.

For just as by one man's disobedience (failing to hear, heedlessness, and carelessness) the many were constituted sinners, so <u>by one Man's obedience the many will be constituted righteous—made acceptable to God, brought into right standing with Him.</u>"
Romans 5:15-19

"How? you say. In Christ. <u>God put the wrong on him who never did anything wrong, so we could be put right with God.</u>"
2 Corinthians 5:21 MSG

2) **The Temptation to "Stumble/Fall"** – At some point during your relationship with God you WILL encounter an opportunity to "stumble/fall" away from living as God directs. This can arise from a former weakness in your sin nature or by outside influences such as satan/others.

3) **This is the CRUCIAL step!** At this point you are at a crossroad with one of two CHOICES to make:

a. to wrongly respond by accepting feelings of frustration, shame, guilt or condemnation by mistakenly believing "My life will never change", "This is TOO hard" or "I guess I'll go back to my old ways." Proverbs 14:14

b. **or** to favorably respond by REPENTING, receiving God's forgiveness and His grace to overcome the offense/obstacle.

> *"If we [freely] admit that we have sinned and confess our sins, He is faithful and just [true to His own nature and promises] and will forgive our sins (dismiss our lawlessness) and continuously cleanse us from all unrighteousness— everything not in conformity to His will purpose, thought and action."*
> I John 1:9

> *"The steps of a [good] man are directed and established by the Lord, when He delights in his way [and He busies Himself with his every step].*
>
> *Though he fall, he shall not be utterly cast down, for the Lord grasps his hand in support and upholds him."*
> Psalm 37:23,24

> *"Rejoice not against me, O my enemy; When I fall, I shall arise; when I sit in darkness, the Lord shall be a light to me."*
> Micah 7:8

4) **"The Pit"** – This is **the wrong response, the destructive reaction** to your thoughts that will spiral you downward into satan's trap. He promotes within you feelings of frustration, despair, shame, guilt and condemnation. His intentionally designed plan is to progressively move you towards thoughts of hopelessness that <u>may eventually</u> lead to thoughts of suicide.

"Maturing in Christ" – This is the **favorable response**, you repent and choose to accept God's forgiveness! You get up and "brush off" your knees realizing God has given you **a new and fresh start** <u>through Jesus Christ</u> for your life! God will also honor you for making the quality choice to proceed onward into the destiny He has ordained for your life!

> *"And be constantly renewed in the spirit of your mind—<u>having a fresh mental and spiritual attitude</u>.*
>
> *And <u>put on the new nature</u> (the regenerate self) created in God's image, <u>(Godlike) in true righteousness and holiness</u>."*
> Ephesians 4:23,24

> *"Do not be conformed to this world—this age, fashioned after and adapted to its external, superficial customs. <u>But be transformed (changed) by the [entire] renewal of your mind—by its new ideals and its new attitude—so that you may prove [for yourselves] what is the good and acceptable and perfect will of God, even the thing which is good and acceptable and perfect [in His sight for you]</u>."*
> Romans 12:2

God has designed you to be an overcomer **NOT** a "quitter!" When you fall, He expects you to call upon Him for assistance and He will be there to help pick you up!

> *"Now to Him Who is able to keep you without stumbling or slipping or falling, and to present [you] unblemished [blameless and faultless] before the presence of His glory—with unspeakable, ecstatic delight—in triumphant joy and exultation,"*
> Jude 1:24

82

"For a righteous man <u>falls seven times and rises again,</u> but the wicked are overthrown by calamity."
Proverbs 24:16

"No matter how many times you trip them up, God-loyal people don't stay down long; Soon they're up on their feet, while the wicked end up flat on their faces."
Proverbs 24:16 MSG

Building a new daily habit

In **Isaiah 55:7-9**, God instructs us to forsake our old, negative, "foul thinking" ways and to change our thoughts to line up with His grand thinking patterns. This is the <u>new</u> lifestyle of a believer! Why do you want to think like God? Because His ways and thoughts are so much higher, grander and more liberating than yours! God requires and desires for you to raise the standard of your thinking up to His level.

You have a daily choice to allow your mind to run loose and unchecked or to make your thoughts subject to your owner, the Lord Jesus Christ.

Begin replacing your old thoughts with God's life-transforming thoughts and perspective of you!

The question for you today is: "What are you thinking about yourself? Are you thinking your way OR God's way?" Are you thinking "I am in right standing with God" <u>or</u> "I am the rejected one?"

As you read earlier about the VCR in your mind, you have a choice each day to stay in the past or to begin enjoying your present and your future. You can trust the Lord! He wants to give you a "brand new VHS tape." It's time to discard the old tape and allow Him to give you a NEW and FRESH attitude.

You decide…

Here are some tremendous truths to begin thinking of to replace the "old VHS tapes" in your mind—Psalms 139:14; Proverbs 31:10; Jeremiah 29:11. These truths record that God has a good plan for your life, and because of Christ your worth is priceless and you are awesomely made! See chapter 25 "Daily Confessions About Myself As God Declares" for additional "new tapes" to place in your thought life. Start building a "new VHS" library in your mind today!

Quality Choice:

Choose to _STOP_ and think about _WHAT_ you think about! Start to challenge yourself to EXCHANGE your thoughts for God's thoughts about yourself, your life, and others. God sees you as His <u>righteous</u> one!

Prescription 3

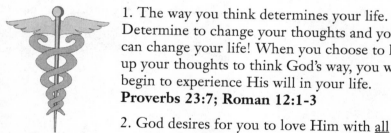

1. The way you think determines your life. Determine to change your thoughts and you can change your life! When you choose to line up your thoughts to think God's way, you will begin to experience His will in your life. **Proverbs 23:7; Roman 12:1-3**

2. God desires for you to love Him with <u>all</u> your heart, mind and strength. He wants to imprint His Words into your mind. Due to the presence of Christ inside of you, you have access to the mind of God and the wisdom of Christ. **Mark 12:30; Hebrews 8:10; 2 Timothy 1:7, Philippians 2:5**

3. God desires for you to align your thoughts to His perspective and purpose for your life. Today He wants to challenge you to "rise up" in your thinking! **Isaiah 55:7-9; Colossians 3:1-10**

4. Face the reality that, as a believer, you are called to a new life! You will need to renew your mind as often as you change your clothes and practice daily hygiene. God promises, you

will get a FRESH and NEW attitude every day when you spend time in His presence and think His Words. **Ephesians 4:17-24; Philippians 4:6-9**

5. According to what you believe (whether positive or negative) you <u>will receive the results of that type of thinking</u>. The thoughts you sow will be the results you receive. Determine to think God's way and receive His peace and power. **Matthew 8:13; Galatians 6:7**

6. Continue reading statements 31-45 in Chapter 25 <u>My Daily Confessions</u>.

Practical Exercises

✔ How do your actions relate to your thoughts? (Romans 8:5)

✔ How will your life be changed when you renew your mind according to God's Word? (Romans 12:2)

✔ How will you know the difference between what is in your mind and what is the mind of God? (2 Corinthians 10:4,5)

✔ How did Jesus Christ counteract satan's words and suggestions? (Matthew 4:1-11)

✔ What type of thinking does the Lord desire for you to fix your mind upon and practice? (Philippians 4:8,9)

Goal – Let us learn to STOP and think about WHAT we're thinking about. You will begin to notice a pattern. You have the choice to change your life starting today!

16

Key 4: You're an Overcomer, Not a "Survivor!" – Exercise Your God Given Authority

---

"My people are destroyed for a lack of knowledge…"
Hosea 4:6

We are destroyed or made "waste" when we do not possess knowledge of God's Word, His revealed truth on the spiritual forces in this world, and our true identity in Jesus Christ. To avoid this destruction we <u>must gain knowledge</u> from God's Word. Then we <u>must apply</u> what we discover!

Areas of Destruction

Domestic abuse and the use of control or manipulation over another individual in ANY form was <u>**NOT**</u> and <u>**IS NOT**</u> God's order for the Christian marriage. **Control** is the root motivator of domestic abuse, where one party possesses a need to exert dominance over the other.

In stark contrast, the Word of God clearly speaks of self-control and self-discipline. You will not find a Scripture where God instructs or authorizes an individual to control another. Self-control is God's plan, while controlling someone else is <u>outside</u> of His plan.

- You are "destroyed" when you fail to know the mutual scope of the marital relationship. From God's perspective, His original plan, and as creations in Jesus Christ, the man and woman are of equal value. They are to exercise mutual submission to one another.

  "Be subject to one another out of reverence for Christ, the Messiah, the Anointed One."
  Ephesians 5:21

- You are "destroyed" when you fail to recognize the reality of spiritual forces operating in this world. The root cause of human battles is based in the spiritual realm.

  "Put on God's whole armor—the armor of a heavy-armed soldier, which God supplies—that you may be able successfully to stand up against [all] the strategies and deceits of the devil.

  "For we are <u>not wrestling</u> with flesh and blood—contending only with physical opponents—<u>but</u> against the despotisms, against the powers, against [the master spirits who are] the world rulers of this present darkness, against the spirit forces of wickedness in the heavenly (supernatural) sphere."
  Ephesians 6:11,12

Satan, (the Bible also identifies him as the devil, the accuser, the father of lies and the deceiver) deploys his hierarchy of demonic spiritual forces to <u>destroy</u> your life <u>or</u> to <u>rob the quality</u> of your existing life!

- You are "destroyed" when you are uninformed <u>or</u> do not accept the truth that satan is a personal enemy whose plan includes keeping people from the liberating truths and lifestyle of Jesus Christ. He is also called the "god of this world."

  "For the god of this world <u>has blinded the unbelievers' minds</u> <u>(that they should not discern the truth), preventing them</u> <u>from seeing</u> the illuminating light of the Gospel of the glory of Christ, the Messiah, Who is the image and likeness of God."
  2 Corinthians 4:4

Once you accept and recognize this truth, the strategies that satan is using in your home and relationships will become crystal clear. As you continue reading, you will discover you are not hopeless, but you can be an "<u>overcomer</u>" through Jesus Christ.

- You are "destroyed" when you are uninformed of your true position and identity in Christ. You unknowingly allow yourself to accept thinking patterns, behaviors, and unhealthy relationships that are outside of God's standard for your life.

"His divine power has given us everything we need for life and godliness through our knowledge of him who called us by his own glory and goodness.

Through these he has given us his very great and precious promises, so that through them you may participate in the divine nature and escape the corruption in the world caused by evil desires.

For this very reason, make every effort to add to your faith goodness; and to goodness, knowledge."
2 Peter 1:3-5 NIV

Let's look at some powerful truths that will open your eyes and change your life today!

Choose to Be on the Winning Team

"When Jesus had received the vinegar, He said, It is finished!"
John 19:30

The Greek word translated "It is finished!" is *tetelestai*. It is a legal connotation meaning "paid in full."[1] On that day He chose to give up His life for you and He triumphed over satan and the forces of evil for all eternity! This historic moment marked the turning of the tide for all mankind, especially for those who believe in Jesus Christ.

For this the Father loves Me, because I lay down My [own] life to take it back again.

No one takes it away from Me. On the contrary, I lay it down voluntarily—I put it from Myself. I am authorized and have power to lay it down—to resign it; and I am authorized and have power to take it back again. These are the instructions (orders) which I have received [as My charge] from My Father.
John 10:17,18

Those words are recorded as a battle cry, a powerful victory cry, as intense as in the heroic movie "Braveheart," when the lead character triumphantly declared in his closing scene, "FREEDOM!"

> *"[God] disarmed the principalities and powers ranged against us and made a bold display and public example of them, in triumphing over them in Him and in it [the cross]."*
> Colossians 2:15

By *His choice* to lay down His life while trusting God would raise Him from the dead, Christ openly **won the victory for you over satan on the cross**. Christ triumphed over satan's plan to control you, and his plan to destroy your life.

How can you celebrate your victory unless you understand the magnitude that His "win" made available for your life? What truly happened when Christ disarmed and triumphed over the evil principalities?

1. Christ reclaimed and took possession of the keys to the gates of Hell and Death. They no longer have control over you when you have accepted Christ. You now have eternal life!

> *"...Do not be afraid! I am the First and the Last,*
>
> *And the Ever Living One—I am living in the eternity of the eternities. I died, but see, I am alive for evermore; and I possess the keys of Death and Hades [the realm of the dead]."*
> Revelation 1:17b,18

> *"Then death and Hades [the state of death or disembodied existence] were thrown into the lake of fire. This is the second death, the lake of fire.*
>
> *And if any one's [name] was not found recorded in the Book of Life, he was hurled into the lake of fire."*
> Revelation 20:14,15

2. Satan and his evil spirits are now also subject to YOU, when you call upon the name of Jesus Christ.

> *"The seventy returned with joy, saying, Lord, even the demons are subject to us in Your name!*
>
> *And He said to them, I saw Satan falling like a lightening [flash] from heaven.*
>
> *Behold! I <u>have given you authority and power</u> to trample upon serpents and scorpions, and (physical and mental strength and ability) over all the power that the enemy (possesses), and nothing shall in any way harm you."*
> Luke 10:17-19

Here is the record of Jesus Christ comforting the twelve disciples prior to His crucifixion. You too can take comfort in the same truth today!

> *"I will not talk with you much more, for the prince (evil genius, ruler) of the world is coming. And he has no claim on Me—he has nothing in common with Me, there is nothing in Me that belongs to him, <u>he has no power over Me</u>."*
> John 14:30

In an attempt to intimidate you, the spirit of control behaves like a "puffer fish" enlarging itself to cause fear in the other party, yet in reality it has no power to harm you! Its fear tactic is attempting to overwhelm you with its temporarily inflated size. <u>It's just a lot of hot air</u>! The spirit of control has **NO** authority over those who know and exercise their rightful authority in Jesus Christ!

3. Satan and his demonic spirits recognize the position and authority of the name of Jesus Christ. They shrink in terror because of Christ's name and its reigning power. They will flee **from you also** when you use His name with the authority He's granted to you.

> *"You believe that God is one; you do well. So do <u>the demons believe, and shudder</u> [in terror and horror such as make a man's hair stand on end and contract the surface of his skin]!"*
> James 2:19

91

4. Christ won complete power and authority over any and all demonic spirits attempting to intimidate or control you. The question is will you choose to accept and then walk in Christ's authority?

Numerous recorded instances show controlling spirits bowed down or fled in Christ's presence. The angry, crazed man who lived in the graveyard and cut himself with stones received deliverance from controlling spirits that possessed his mind (Mark 5:2-19). The young boy controlled by the spirit, which caused him to convulse and throw his body into fires, was set free when Christ came upon the scene (Matthew 17:14-20; Luke 9:38-43).

5. Christ won all authority, all power, and supreme headship when He triumphed at the cross for YOU! You share and can live daily in the same victory when you remind satan and yourself that he is a "defeated devil, a defeated opponent" who no longer has any right to steal, kill or destroy the quality of your God-given life!

"Far above all rule and authority and power and dominion, and every name that is named—above every title that can be conferred—not in this age and in this world, but also in the age and the world which are to come.

And He has put <u>all</u> things under His feet and has appointed Him <u>the universal and supreme Head</u> of the church (a headship exercised throughout the church)."
Ephesians 1:21,22

Christ is the "undisputed Champion of the Universe!" The question is will <u>you</u> choose to honor His title and walk in the authority He has given you?

He makes you a winner and you have nothing to fear! God handpicked you for the winning team when you accepted Christ. You are His "first round" pick, specifically chosen for His team. Now your responsibility is to accept that truth!

What is Christ speaking to your heart today about your life? What is the challenge or hurdle in front of you? Trust Him; allow Him to take you up and over, directly across your victory line. Greater is He that is in you than he that is in the world!

> *"Little children, you are of God—you belong to Him—and have [already] defeated and overcome them [the agents of antichrist] because He Who lives in you is greater (mightier) than he who is in the world."*
> 1 John 4:4

You are an OVERCOMER, because of Jesus Christ's decisive victory over satan, his demonic forces and his evil ways. Choose to follow your Captain's leadership and He'll lead you through into daily victories!

Winning Team Benefits

1. Winners sit on the same side.

> *"And He raised us up together with Him and made us sit down together—giving us joint seating with Him—in the heavenly sphere [by virtue of our being] in Christ Jesus, the Messiah, the Anointed One."*
> Ephesians 2:6

2. The teammates know they have the victory because of the leader's proven track record!

> *"For whatsoever is born of God is victorious over the world; and this is the victory that conquers the world, even our faith.*
>
> *Who is it that is victorious over (that conquers) the world but he who believes that Jesus is the Son of God—who adheres to, trusts in and relies [on that fact]?"*
> I John 5:4,5

3. Jesus Christ never lost a battle, and we win by being on His team.

> *"Yet amid all these things we are now more than conquerors and gain a surpassing victory through Him Who loved us."*
> Romans 8:37

"Conqueror" is the Greek word "Hupernikeo," it means to have *more* than a victory. You have *more than* a victory when you follow Christ's instructions for your life.

4. Victory brings privileges and bestowed rights. Jesus Christ bestows His authority on you to take charge over all demonic spirits.

"Then Jesus called together the twelve apostles, and gave them power and authority over all demons and to cure diseases."
Luke 9:1

The word "authority" is the Greek word "exousia," meaning, "exercised privilege, legal power to enforce."

Overcoming Controlling Behaviors

If your marital relationship is severely eroded, the required prescription is <u>intensive care</u> and <u>correction</u> from the Word of God.

If your personality is to run and hide, even though the Lord is instructing you to lovingly confront someone, here are some words of insight: the sole standard and direction for our lives is the Word of God! It clearly teaches us how to get back on track when the issues of life take us astray (2 Timothy 3:16). You are on the winning team when you accept Christ into your life. You have access to His authority and privileges when you speak and act using His name.

You can take authority over controlling evil spirits in the name of Jesus Christ. Seek the Lord's direction and wisdom then He will guide your steps. For some of you, He may direct you to confront your spouse. The Lord will give you the words and the best manner in which to communicate (1 Peter 3:1). When someone has been a controller for a long time they will NOT readily receive your message. You are responsible to share only what the Lord is prompting in your heart; you are NOT responsible for their reaction to the message!

Since Genesis 3:7-17 with the "fall of mankind," when people are confronted with the light of truth, their natural response includes hiding, shifting blame, making excuses, and unwillingness to accept responsibility for their actions.

The same behaviors exist today in a co-dependent marriage. The offender abuses while the recipient hides the offensive acts, excuses and justifies or rationalizes the inappropriate behavior.

The main reason we don't confront spouses or others about inappropriate behavior is because we are more concerned about our personal "comfort zone" than with helping the other person mature! Your mind and feelings say, "It's inconvenient for me, uncomfortable for me, I'm afraid of what they will say, or they may reject me."

The reality is, when you give in to people, you're actually **hindering** them and you sadly contribute to feeding their inappropriate behaviors. Consequently you have stunted their growth opportunity and you are buffering them from the accountability and consequences of their POOR behavior. Inappropriate behaviors need to be addressed directly, yet with love, because that is the exact way God relates to His people.

> *"A man of great wrath shall suffer the penalty; for if you deliver him [from the consequences], he will [feel free to] cause you to do it again."*
> Proverbs 19:19

Do not be surprised when you encounter resistance as you begin confronting these long-term inappropriate behaviors with your newfound confidence. You must first pray, asking the Lord for His wisdom, then follow through as He directs. The Holy Spirit will inspire you with the best words at the best time. Then it's up to you to follow His prompting.

Do not be caught off guard if you receive resistant reactions. Hold fast to your ground and follow the Captain's (Jesus Christ's) directions and you will see the fruits of your obedience.

If your situation is one where physical danger is imminent, please find the safe shelter of a family member, neighbor, local church, or a friend. **The Lord never requires you to place your life in harm's way!** You have the right to a safe place and are entitled to set healthy

God-given boundaries until the behavior of the other party demonstrates notable and measurable positive changes. Romans 13:1-6 declares, God has ordained earthly authorities to correct and penalize evil behaviors of those who choose to rebel. You must recognize you are too valuable and priceless to His team to accept physical abuse!

Whatever Jesus Christ is directing you to do, you must realize He entitles you to His authority, His protection, His power, and the spiritual authority to follow through with the instruction.

> *You shall __not__ fear them, for the Lord your God shall fight for you.*
> Deuteronomy 3:22

> *For God __did not__ give us a spirit of timidity—of cowardice, of craven and cringing and fawning fear—but [He has given us a spirit] of power and of love and of a calm and well-balanced mind and discipline and self-control.*
> 2 Timothy 1:7

As a Christian woman filled with the presence of Jesus Christ and the Holy Spirit, you were not designed to passively tolerate some of the atrocities placed upon you. Instead God designed for you to be an OVERCOMER, successfully equipped with His truth. You do not need to accept or tolerate behaviors, which the righteousness (right living, right standing with God) of God does not accept! You were made to be the righteousness of God and to walk in God-given authority, freedom, and power!

Let us learn from the warning Isaiah declared:

> *"Woe to those who call evil good and good evil, who put darkness for light and light for darkness, who put bitter for sweet and sweet for bitter."*
> Isaiah 5:20

As a woman of God filled with the Holy Spirit, it is your God-given responsibility to acknowledge and respond to what God has spoken. You are accountable to hold to the standard of God's Word in your family, in your home and in your life. **You are not to condone behaviors which God condemns as evil!**

> *The reverent fear and worshipful awe of the Lord includes the hatred of evil.*
> Proverbs 8:13a

The Word of God is your "Bill of Rights" clearly defining the rights God has entitled to you and your family.

Please consider these closing truths:

You **are responsible** to follow through as the Scripture records and the Holy Spirit directs.

You **are not responsible** or accountable for the other person's response!

You **can only** change yourself!

You **cannot** change someone else!

As YOU change yourself, the other person will change. Why? Because you have changed the stimuli to which they are to respond. (If YOU change, the other person must respond accordingly to your change.)

You **can pray for God to "open their eyes"** so the offender may see and discover the better way of living (Ephesians 1:18; 2 Timothy 2:25,26).

Quality Choice:

Recognize you are an OVERCOMER through Jesus Christ! When you accepted Him into your heart, He placed you on the winning team, entitling you to all of His rights and privileges. The Bible is your "Bill of Rights" defining God's standards of excellence for your life. Choose to accept your granted authority from Christ.

Prescription 4

1. Your daily battles are not with "flesh and blood." They are battles caused by spiritual entities. To effectively gain the victory, you must use spiritual tactics. **John 16:33; Ephesians 6:10-17**

2. Jesus Christ openly disarmed satan; proclaimed the victory over satan, and made him ineffective when He went to the cross. Christ took total authority over satan at Calvary. **Romans 6:13,14; Colossians 2:15, Revelations 1:17-19**

3. Jesus Christ overcame death for you, so you can enjoy eternal life with Him. **Revelations 1:17-19; Revelations 20:13-15**

4. Due to the presence of Christ in you, you have His authority over satan and nothing will harm you when you claim your authority in Jesus Christ's name. You have the upper hand in life with Christ. Follow His direction. **Luke 10:17-20; Luke 11:20-23; James 2:19; Romans 6:9-14**

5. Continue reading statements 46-60 in Chapter 25 <u>My Daily Confessions</u>

Practical Exercise

✔ Ask the Holy Spirit to reveal to you the areas in your life where you need to appropriate Christ's authority.

✔ In a journal, note those areas brought to your attention and the date.

✔ Ask the Holy Spirit to help you exercise Christ's delegated authority in the revealed areas. Then choose to follow His instruction.

✔ Once completed, log the results of following His instruction. You <u>will</u> begin to experience Jesus Christ's pattern of success by exercising your "Bill of Rights."

17

Key 5: Are You Ready for Renewal?

"Teacher, which is the greatest commandment in the Law?

Jesus replied: Love the Lord your God with all your heart and with all your soul and with all your mind. This is the first and greatest commandment."
Matthew 22:36,37 NIV

"Keep your heart with all vigilance and above all that you guard, for out of it flow the springs of life."
Proverbs 4:23

The condition or quality of the human heart is vitally important to God. He desires for us to love Him first with our <u>whole</u> heart, our <u>entire</u> mind and every fiber of our being.

It is out of the human heart from which we make life decisions. If your heart is troubled or shaken, you will make a decision based on its troubled or shaken condition. Similarly, when your heart is fixed and at rest, you will make decisions from a basis of peace.

When you're in an abusive situation, you spend more time thinking, battling, and struggling with satan (through others) instead of spending time with God and enjoying His peace. Your mind's attention is overwhelmed by trying to change the other person, trying to figure out the situation, or in some cases, trying to "survive" mentally, emotionally, or physically. This is satan's deceptive tactic of distracting you from God by creating a situation to wear you down! His ultimate goal is to cause you to feel weary, eventually helpless and ultimately hopeless in your heart.

"Wear down" means to break down the resistance of by relentless pressure, hence wear down the opposition.[1]

Satan's goal is to completely exhaust you—mentally, emotionally, physically and spiritually.

God in His tremendous forethought for you designed a way for you to get a FRESH start and outlook each day!

> *"Do not be conformed to this world—this age, fashioned after and adapted to its external, superficial customs. But be transformed (changed) by the [entire] renewal of your mind—by its new ideals and its new attitude—so that you may prove [for yourselves] what is that good and acceptable and perfect will of God, even the thing which is good and acceptable and perfect [in His sight for you]. "*
> Romans 12:2

What happens when you daily renew your mind in God's Word and to His way of thinking and perceiving life? You get refreshed, and renewed, like when you drink a cool, tall glass of water on a humid summer day.

The Greek word for renew is <u>anakaino</u> which means "new in quality."

Knowing life can wear us down, God intentionally designed for the batteries of your heart and mind to be recharged with "a new quality" by His presence every day.

If your mind and life have been turned upside down like mine was, you will need to run to the Lord almost minute by minute for a *fresh attitude*. Allow Him to safely guide you and the decisions of your heart.

God **is** concerned and **cares** about your heart. To Him it is the most defining component of your character.

> *"But the Lord said to Samuel, Look not on his appearance or at the height of his stature, for I have rejected him; for the Lord sees not as man sees; for man looks on the outward appearance, but the Lord looks on the heart."*
> I Samuel 16:7

Jesus Christ asks you to come to Him for regular refreshment and renewal. Without it you will experience various levels of "burnout."

100

"Come to Me, all you who labor and are heavy-laden and over burdened, and I will give you to rest—I will ease and relieve and refresh your souls.

Take My yoke upon you, and learn of Me; for I am gentle (meek) and humble (lowly) in heart, and you will find rest—relief, ease and refreshment and recreation and blessed quiet—for your souls."
Matthew 11:28,29

Since the heart is the determining factor of the quality of one's character and life, God desires for it to operate at peak condition, which is a "pure" heart before Him. As recorded in Matthew 5:8, it is only when you bring Him your emptied heart, that you will be able to see God and experience an intimate relationship with Him.

Matthew 12:34 and Matthew 15:17-19, shows us that the thoughts, words, and actions you manifest ALWAYS originate from the contents of your heart! <u>If you want to change your outward responses, ask the Holy Spirit to help you change the contents of your heart.</u>

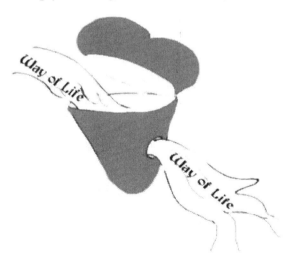

You **can** change the "outflow" of your life when you change the "input" of your heart. The original ingredients you pour into your heart will determine its corresponding outflow. Your life can flow in the way of life **or** the way of death.

101

"As in water face reflects face, So the heart of man reflects man."
Proverbs 27:19 NAS

The condition of the heart reflects the TRUE nature of a person. If you really want to know a person, make it a point to spend time with them. Ask God to reveal their true character (which emanates from the heart) to you.

The Benefits of Heart Renewal

You may ask why is it so important to spend time in ensuring that your heart is renewed? We discovered earlier that it is out of the heart where you make life decisions. As an engine drives a car, similarly your heart drives the direction of your life. If it's in poor running condition—tattered, torn, hardened—you will be in for a rough ride. If it's fresh and new, you can enjoy a smoother ride even on rough terrain!

Due to our original sin nature, the heart is inherently "faulty" and <u>requires</u> regular maintenance from the Lord.

Jeremiah 17:9,10 records–due to the natural perversity of the heart, it benefits us to bring it regularly before the Lord. He is the one who knows, who tries and can purify the unclean things from within it.

"The heart is deceitful above all things, and it is exceedingly perverse and corrupt and severely, mortally sick! Who can know it [perceive, understand, be acquainted with his own heart and mind]? I, the Lord search the mind, I try the heart, even to give every man according to his ways, according to the fruit of his doings."

The condition of your heart determines your degree of intimacy or fellowship with the Lord. When your heart is responsive to the leading of the Lord and His Word, you will make sound choices. When your heart is troubled, fearful, or in disarray, you typically make unsound choices. Therefore it makes sense to regularly go to God for heart maintenance checks.

"Search me [thoroughly], O God, and know my heart! Try me, and know my thoughts!

And see if there is any wicked or hurtful way in me, and lead me in the way everlasting."
Psalms 139:23,24

During one of those heart reflecting quiet times with the Lord, He lovingly yet firmly revealed to me, "Michele, during the past few months you have become an idolater!" I said, "Oh, no Lord not me! Where? How?" He then explained, "You have **spent so much time** thinking about your husband, placing him on a pedestal, trying to fix the situation on your own and battling your own imaginations in the relationship that your face **has turned completely from** Me. That is why you are so tired! Make a choice today to release all your thoughts, and issues over to Me! Turn your attention back to Me!"

His heart piercing truth went straight to my core. I wept with remorse and repentance for some time, while asking Jesus Christ to forgive me and the Holy Spirit to give me strength to receive it.

At that very moment, a weight lifted from my heart! I experienced a lightness I had not felt in a long time. From that moment I began looking forward to my daily scheduled "heart checkups" with the Lord. I realized that spending time in His presence would yield innumerable benefits!

The book of Psalms reveals that numerous heart changes can be expected by spending time and pouring out your heart before Jesus Christ. You can expect several positive results when your heart is open and honest before the Lord. To name a few: you can expect a <u>clean</u> heart (devoid of issues which clog your heart), a <u>strong</u> heart, and a <u>fearless</u> heart.

Proverbs 14:30 explains there are *immediate and long-term* benefits in undergoing regular heart renewal from the Lord: a calm and undisturbed mind and heart bring life and health to your body!

"Those whom I [dearly and tenderly] love, I tell their faults and convict and convince and reprove and chasten—[that is] I discipline and instruct them. So be enthusiastic and in earnest and burning with zeal and repent—changing your mind and attitude."
Revelation 3:19

What "rough or worn" spots are currently weighing down your heart? What deceptive battles are you fighting today which are wearing your heart down from your personal relationship with Jesus Christ? Ask the Holy Spirit to reveal these truths to you. As recorded in John 8:32, *"You shall know the truth and it shall make you free."*

Quality Choice:

Like our Lord Jesus Christ, choose to regularly make time with God for your heart to be maintained. Renewal time with Him will comfort, strengthen, and refresh you. Establish a daily "date" time with your Lord Jesus Christ.

Prescription 5

1. When you spend time with the Lord your strength will be renewed, your stamina and energy level will increase. **Isaiah 40:31; Psalms 103:4,5**

2. Without spending time with the Lord, you are more vulnerable to satan's attacks. **I Peter 5:6-10**

3. Ask God to help you keep Him at the center of your heart and your life's decisions. **Proverbs 4:21-23**

4. The greatest commandment is to love the Lord your God with all your heart. It is God's desire to remove anything in your life that is hindering your relationship with Him. **Matthew 22:37,38**

5. You can receive a fresh start each day as you spend time with God. **2 Corinthians 4:16; Ephesians 4:22-24; Colossians 3:5-11**

6. Continue reading statements 61-75 in Chapter 25 <u>My Daily Confessions</u>.

Practical Exercises

Suggestions for Renewal Time:

✔ Spend time with God in His Word (Bible, books, tapes).

✔ Take long nature walks—in a park, in the mountains, or near a lake.

✔ Listen to God-inspired music.

✔ Take a relaxing bath with candles.

✔ Just as the Psalmist sought God, you too can ask the Lord to change your heart.

> *"Let the words of my mouth and the meditation of my heart be acceptable in Your sight, O Lord, my [firm, impenetrable] rock and my redeemer."*
> Psalms 19:14

✔ During your renewal time, ask the Holy Spirit to help you discover the motive, purpose and intent of <u>your</u> heart choices with these questions:

- What within your heart <u>initially attracted you</u> to your mate?

- What caused you to <u>choose to marry</u> your mate?

- What caused you to <u>overlook the first occurrence</u> of inappropriate behavior?

- What caused you <u>to continue</u> to excuse, rationalize, tolerate or cover up <u>the repeated</u> inappropriate behaviors?

- Prior to this time, what caused you to avoid, admit or deny the truth that these inappropriate behavior patterns <u>are contrary to the will of God</u> for the Christian marriage?

> *"Behold, You desire truth in the inner being; make me therefore to know wisdom in my inmost heart."*
> Psalms 51:6

Key 6: Drop Your Load, Turn in Your Shopping Cart (The Power of Forgiveness)

Are you a "bag" woman?

Have you ever toured around a big city? Maybe New York, Philadelphia, Chicago, or even Los Angeles?

Imagine yourself enjoying the skyline, the gleaming buildings, the sights, and sounds, then you see "that person" wandering in your direction with their head down pushing some type of cart. In New York they are referred to as "bag" women or men. Their shopping carts are heavily weighed down with items collected from their past and present. If for any reason the wind blows an item or the person mistakenly drops an item, they will quickly turn around to make sure they have retrieved their material, and stuff it back into the cart. They will protect their possessions at any cost.

Unfortunately, many of us live our lives in the same fashion. We may dwell in sophisticated cities or nice homes, yet spiritually, mentally, and emotionally we are walking "bag people" carrying old burdens, secret sins, and the oppression of shame, guilt, and condemnation.

Well, today the Lord is extending an invitation for you to drop **your** baggage and receive His freedom through Jesus Christ!

To proceed with this chapter, you must first recognize that you cannot **receive or extend forgiveness** by sheer human will power. Forgiveness is not inherently included within the human or "flesh" component of mankind. **You must call and choose to rely upon the GRACE of God and the Holy Spirit to empower and enable you to forgive yourself and others**.

Forgiving Yourself

Secret sins, behaviors of the past, poor choices you have made, and hurts you have inflicted upon others will weigh you down, hindering you from freely relating to God. Yet God knew satan would use unforgiveness to make you feel ashamed, unworthy, or "dirty" before God. The Heavenly Father set a plan in place for your relationship with Him to be restored, renewed, and rekindled. All you need to do is ask for His forgiveness...

> "If we [freely] admit that we have sinned and confess our sins, He is faithful and just [true to His nature and promises] and will forgive our sins (dismiss our lawlessness) and continuously cleanse us from all unrighteousness—everything not in conformity to His will in purpose, thought and action."
> I John 1:9

In the book of Psalms 103:2-4,11,12 God declares, when you go to Him, He forgives all your iniquities, He takes back your life from the pit and destruction then He beautifies and dignifies your life with loving kindness.

Learn to shake off guilt, condemnation, and unrighteousness— they just weigh you down! God forgives and pardons you when you ask for it. If God forgives you, isn't it time for you to forgive and forget the offenses too?

> "He then goes on to say, And their sins and their lawbreakings I will remember no more."
> Hebrews 10:17

While I was seeking the Lord during my restoration, the Holy Spirit revealed that my mind wrongfully harbored the thought that our marriage had ended because of my youthful indiscretions. I thought, "You deserve this, you brought this upon yourself! It's your punishment! Now you must live with it!"

The Holy Spirit reminded me, "Michele, God forgave you twenty years ago when you asked, yet you failed *to receive* it on your end!" At that moment, I asked the Lord to help me. I cried out, "Yes Lord, I accept your forgiveness!" Inside I experienced a warm washing that flowed from my head to my feet. The tears rolled down my face, and like a joyful child, I felt clean, released, and FREE!

The Apostle Paul consented to and petitioned for the murder of countless Christians. Yet Paul chose to RECEIVE God's gift of forgiveness and he continued on to become the greatest apostle in history! The Lord wants to set you free today! Give your secret, unspoken issue(s) to Him. We can learn of the Lord's grace and mercy from David. Months after committing adultery, premeditated murder and treason against a loyal soldier, David realized the weight of his unconfessed sin.

> *"Blessed—Happy, fortunate [to be envied]—is he who has forgiveness of his transgression continually exercised upon him, whose sin is covered.*
>
> *Blessed—happy, fortunate, [to be envied]—is the man to whom the Lord imputes no iniquity, and in whose spirit there is no deceit.*
>
> *When I kept silence [before I confessed], my bones wasted away through my groaning all the day long.*
>
> *For day and night Your hand [of displeasure] was heavy upon me; my moisture was turned into the drought of summer. Selah [pause, and calmly think of that]!*
>
> *I acknowledge my sin to You, and my iniquity I did not hide. I said, I will confess my transgressions to the Lord [continually unfolding the past till all is told] then You [instantly] forgave me the guilt and iniquity of my sin. Selah [pause, and calmly think of that]!"*
> Psalms 32:1-5

Name your offense (adultery, promiscuity, drugs, abortions, out of wedlock children, prostitution, lying, cheating, stealing, and countless others). God's mercy, grace, and endless love for you **far outweigh** the offense. His forgiveness is available for you today! Make the choice to ASK for forgiveness and God will meet you. Your ultimate responsibility is to accept or RECEIVE His forgiveness!

"Come now, and let us reason together, says the Lord;
though your sins be as scarlet, they shall be as white as snow;
though they be red like crimson, they shall be as wool."
Isaiah 1:18

When you decide to repent and ask for the Lord's forgiveness, <u>He</u> cleanses you of <u>all</u> your past sins and transgressions. Bring your sins to Jesus Christ. He alone can save and <u>completely</u> free you from a "stained" past (Hebrews 7:25)!

Colossians 2:13-15 shows that when God forgives you through the blood of Jesus Christ, your former sins are "paid in full" and you **no longer** owe a debt to anyone (which includes yourself). You are "free and clear" to move forward with an unburdened heart and enjoy a sweet relationship with the Lord.

Note: Upon extending forgiveness to you, God no longer remembers the matter. If and when the matter arises in the future, please know the accusation is coming from satan and not from God!

Jesus Christ paid the debt (tab) for your sin in full, free and clear! It is a waste of your time and effort to mistakenly think <u>you</u> could pay the tab a second time! Accept God's gift of forgiveness by learning to "shake off" the accusations, accept His righteousness and keep moving forward with your life! Decide to <u>not</u> look back.

Quality Choice:

Choose to stop critically judging yourself! When you sin, go boldly to the throne of grace and ask for God's forgiveness. Once you've repented, get back up and continue walking in relationship with Him.

Prescription 6

1. When your inner self is downcast or disquieted bring the matter to God. He can help change your disposition. **Psalms 43:5**

2. Every one of your sins, shortcomings, and transgressions can be forgiven when you bring them before God. He does not keep accusing you or shamefully reminding you of them. **Psalms 86:5; Psalms 103:3,8-10**

3. God forgets your sin once you receive His forgiveness and He removes it so far away that it may no longer touch you. **Psalms 103:12; Isaiah 43:25; Micah 7:18,19**

4. The blood of Jesus Christ cleanses sin away from you and restores your relationship to God. **Ephesians 1:7; Colossians 1:13,14**

5. After you have received God's forgiveness, accept it, and choose to no longer judge yourself. Then move on with the plan God has for your life. **I Corinthians 4:3,4**

Practical Exercises

✔ What secret thoughts/actions/situations are weighing you down right now? Ask the Holy Spirit to help you identify them.

Whatever they are, bring them to the Lord. Bring each matter to His altar and allow Him to forgive AND thoroughly cleanse you. Before you leave His presence remember to **receive** your forgiveness!

Forgiving Others

You may be thinking, "Does this mean I should forgive my spouse or ex-spouse?" You must be kidding me! After all the chaos and hell I've been through, why should I forgive? How can I forgive?"

I understand your pain. The thought of forgiveness brought a lump to my throat and a sting to my soul. You may be thinking right now about closing this book. **Just hold on and read further before you make that decision!** This guidebook is about healing and overcoming. It's about getting rid of the unseen bondages of the soul and heart that will eventually destroy your entire life.

Why forgive others? Let's look at the benefits:

> *"For it is not an enemy who reproaches and taunts me; then I might bear it; nor one who has hated me who insolently vaunts himself against me; then I might hide from him.*
>
> *But it was you, a man my equal, my companion and my familiar friend;*
>
> *We had sweet fellowship together, and used to walk to the house of God in company.*
>
> *[My companion] has put forth his hands against those who were at peace with him; he has broken and profaned his agreement [of friendship and loyalty].*
>
> *The words of his mouth were smoother than cream or butter, but war was in his heart; his words were softer than oil, yet they were drawn swords."*
> Psalms 55:12-14,20,21

King David's words powerfully and accurately described the hurt, shock, depth of betrayal, and pain I experienced in the deterioration of my marriage.

The one person I prayed for, longed for, and the only one I shared the innermost part of my heart's dreams had become a stranger and my enemy! Although he spoke with smooth words, his actions were those of someone at war with me. I was taken off guard, stunned and reeled from staggering disbelief! How did we get to this point?

I had to make a choice! I cried out: "Lord, help me!"

He showed me that I could: allow unforgiveness to settle in my heart and become a bitter, hardened woman who would eventually die from the inside out **or** I could choose to release the person and offenses to the Lord.

The Holy Spirit alone could help release the chains that unforgiveness placed on my heart, mind, and life. His help released me to again enjoy a FREE relationship with God. His help later empowered me to write a letter to my former spouse expressing responsibility for areas in the marriage where I could have been a better mate. I concluded the letter by wishing him success in his life journey.

It seemed within moments after mailing the letter, I actually felt lighter on the inside. I felt genuine freedom and my thoughts became clear! For the first time in months, since the divorce my mind and heart felt totally free!

> *"And whenever you stand praying, if you have anything against any one, forgive him and let it drop—leave it, let it go—in order that your Father Who is in Heaven may also forgive you your [own] failings and shortcomings and let them drop.*
>
> *But if you do not forgive, neither will your Father in heaven forgive your failings and shortcomings."*
> Mark 11:25,26

Lack of forgiveness actually produces a "tormenting weight" of oppression within your soul and prevents you from enjoying other relationships in life (family, friends, co-workers, etc.) Most importantly, **you won't** enjoy your relationship with your Heavenly Father.

Imagine yourself tying a chain around **your** neck, yet you expect the "unforgiven" person to choke! This is unreasonable, yet we do this every day. You're the one holding onto unforgiveness, your mind keeps replaying the offense and your life becomes tangled in knots. Meanwhile, the unsuspecting "unforgiven" person is moving on, enjoying their life. They're totally unaware or unconcerned about the thoughts you're holding against them. You have now choked up **your** mind and life while they're the "happy campers"! Is this sound logic to you?

The main reason God designed forgiveness is to release **you** of inner bondage! Unforgiveness creates an invisible torment on your soul, slowly choking you to death on the inside and ultimately hindering you from moving freely on the outside.

During women's conferences to demonstrate this truth about inner bondage, I ask one of the participants to assist me by recounting the offenses, which she held against others. Each time she recalled an offense, a piece of 12-foot chain was wrapped around one of her body parts. By the time she finished we saw her bound from neck to ankles. Then I asked her to walk back to her seat. Of course she couldn't. She had to hop back because the weight of the chain on her body was too heavy and restricted her from moving freely.

Jesus Christ explained this truth:

> *"Then his master called him and said to him, You contemptible and wicked attendant! I forgave and cancelled all that [great] debt of yours because you begged me;*
>
> *And should you not have had pity and mercy on your fellow attendant, as I had pity and mercy on you?*
>
> *And in wrath his master turned him over to the torturers (the jailers), till he should pay all that he owed.*
>
> *So also My heavenly Father will deal with every one of you, if you do not freely forgive your brother from your heart his offenses."*
> Matthew 18:32-35

When we choose not to forgive, we are the ones who actually go into bondage. We are given over to the "tormentors" of life. The offender goes along his merry way, most of the time clueless and unaffected by your unforgiveness, while you are left bound by your choice. Consequently the other areas of your life slowly yet steadily become weighed down and infected by unforgiveness. How? The chains of torment, the "oppressive weight" of unforgiveness negatively impacts your thoughts, words, perceptions and consequently **your** treatment of others. This ultimately robs you of **your** quality of life.

Most people can recall someone they know who died still impacted by the ugly imprint of bitterness, anger, regret, and loneliness on their soul. Sadly they chose to carry the bondage of unforgiveness to their grave.

Other Benefits Of Forgiveness

- Forgiveness keeps the "pipeline" open, free of hindrances between you and God.

  "And forgive us our debts, as we also have forgiven (left, remitted and let go of the debts, and given up resentment against) our debtors.

  And lead (bring) us not into temptation, but deliver us from the evil one. For Yours is the kingdom and the power and glory forever. Amen.

  For if you forgive people their trespasses—that is, their reckless and willful sins, leaving them, letting them go, and giving up resentment—<u>your heavenly Father will also forgive you</u>.

  But if you do not forgive others their trespasses—that is, their reckless an d willful sins, leaving them, letting them go and giving up resentment—<u>neither will your Father forgive you your trespasses</u>."
  Matthew 6:12-15

- Forgiveness keeps you free from the devices (being entrapped) of satan.

  "If you forgive any one anything, I too forgive that one; and what I have forgiven, if I have forgiven anything, has been for your sakes in the presence [and with the approval] of Christ, the Messiah,

  To keep Satan from getting the advantage over us; for we are not ignorant of his wiles and intentions."
  II Corinthians 2:10,11

- Forgiveness prevents satan from having an advantage over your life and eroding its quality.

Finally unforgiveness implies you have a burning desire to *"make them pay"* for the offenses committed knowingly or unknowingly against you. The collection or extraction of payment for perceived injustices in life is not your responsibility!

The largest debt, (the wages of sin is death) is paid in full when you accept Jesus Christ. From that moment on, you no longer owe a debt to God Almighty. Who am I to not forgive someone, when God has erased *my* debts and forgiven me?

> *"And become useful and helpful and kind to one another,*
> *tenderhearted (compassionate, understanding, loving*
> *hearted), forgiving one another [readily and freely], as God*
> *in Christ forgave you."*
> Ephesians 4:32

The ultimate responsibility in the measuring of justice is to be done by the Lord. His Sovereign laws dictate that what we sow is what we will reap. We each will bear the "fruit of our actions" whether they are good or bad.

> *"For we know Him Who said, Vengeance is Mine—*
> *retribution and the meting out of full justice rest with Me; I*
> *will repay—I will exact the compensation, says the Lord.*
> *And again, The Lord will judge and determine and solve*
> *and settle the cause and the cases of His people.*
>
> *It is a fearful (formidable and terrible) thing to incur the*
> *divine penalties and be cast into the hands of the living God!"*
> Hebrews 10:30,31

God will be the one to repay for anyone's injustice! He wants you to move on, enjoy your life, and allow Him to deal with the offender.

"Hurting" People Hurt Other People

Due to the fallen, sinful nature of mankind as recorded in Genesis 3, "hurting" people **will** hurt other people! This truth is evidenced throughout the generations of mankind. Domestic abuse is a generational behavior. The destructive behaviors and damaging effects of domestic abuse will continue into the next generation UNTIL someone makes a quality choice to break the cycle by changing their path to follow God's way of living.

*"I call Heaven and earth to witness this day against you,
that I have set before you life and death, the blessings and
the curses; therefore choose life, that you and your
descendants may live."*
Deuteronomy 30:19

Studies show children raised in abusive homes are more likely to marry abusive mates or become an abuser. The cycle of sin with its bitter effects <u>will break when one person chooses to enter into a vital relationship with Jesus Christ</u>! Choosing His way of life changes the path for you and your children.

Unless you allow the Lord to heal, cleanse, and renew your heart, you TOO may pass your hurt, anger, bitterness, and shame on to the next generation. Today, make a quality choice to submit to the Lord's prescribed means of healing and overcoming your situation!

In the Meantime...Chose to Live in Peace

*"Repay no one evil for evil, but take thought for what is
honest and proper and noble—aiming to be above
reproach—in the sight of every one.*

*If possible, as far as it depends on you, live at peace with
every one.*

*Beloved, never avenge yourselves, but leave the way open for
[God's] wrath; for it is written, Vengeance is Mine, I will
repay (requite), says the Lord.*

*But, if your enemy is hungry, feed him; if he is thirsty, give
him drink; for by so doing you will heap burning coals upon
his head.*

*Do not let yourself be overcome by evil, but overcome
(master) evil with good."*
Romans 12:17-21

Your time on earth is precious. Each day we must choose to use our time **wisely** to maximize our remaining moments on earth.

In Romans 12:18, the Lord directs us to live in peace as much as lies within our responsibility. Instead of repaying evil with evil, we are instructed to walk on the higher ground and do the noble thing. Know that God fairly administers justice for injustices. Your relationships can also improve when you choose to do good towards those who have offended you. Your kind ways can cause them to warm up and **you** will overcome evil.

Quality Choice:

Set YOURSELF free by choosing to release the offender to God, ensuring your prayers and relationship with God remains unhindered.

Prescription 6A

1. Releasing unforgiveness ensures your relationship with God remains unhindered. **Matthew 6:12-15**

2. Releasing unforgiveness keeps you free of satan's entrapments in your life. **II Corinthians 2:9-11**

3. Taking the higher ground will cause you to overcome evil in life. **Romans 12:17-21**

4. The Lord will avenge and repay you for the injustices you have endured. **Hebrews 10:30,31**

Practical Exercises

Eight practical steps to healing bitterness:

1. Choose to become willing to forgive.

2. Ask the Holy Spirit to enable you. You cannot do it in your own strength.

3a. Make a list of all the things people have done to hurt or offend you (Item A).

3b. Make a list of everything YOU HAVE done to offend God (Item B).

4a. Write Matthew 18:21,22 across "Item A."

4b. Write I John 1:9 across "Item B."

5. Then take BOTH of the lists and TEAR THEM UP!!!

6. Make a final list (Item C) of the positive things that have come from this negative situation in your life. (Read the life of Joseph recorded in Genesis chapters 37-50.)

7. Pray for those who offended you. Luke 6:27,28

8. Determine to STOP SPEAKING ABOUT THE OFFENSE. Choose instead to BLESS the offender. Romans 12:14; Proverbs 17:9

19

Key 7: Stay Clear! Danger Zone Ahead! Avoiding Strife, Bitterness, Anger and Resentment

Some of us were raised in a household where strife, bitterness, anger, and resentment commonly displayed themselves. Others learned those behaviors later in life. Regardless, once you accept Jesus Christ as your Savior and Lord, His new nature and temperament are now available to you.

> *"The Lord is gracious and full of compassion, slow to anger and abounding in mercy and loving-kindness."*
> Psalms 145:8

> *"You have been regenerated—born again—not from a mortal origin (seed, sperm) but from one that is immortal by the ever living and lasting Word of God."*
> 1 Peter 1:23

> *"No one born (begotten) of God [deliberately, knowingly] habitually practices sin, <u>for God's nature abides in him—His principle of life, the divine sperm, remains permanently within him</u>—and he cannot practice sinning because he is born (begotten) of God."*
> I John 3:9

> *"For by these He has granted to us His precious and magnificent promises, so that by them you may become <u>partakers of the divine nature</u>, having escaped the corruption that is in the world by lust."*
> 2 Peter 1:4 NAS

The very nature of God, your Heavenly Father, is "slow to anger." As a child of God born from His incorruptible seed and given His nature, you now have the same nature within your spirit! You are now the one who chooses to exercise your new nature. Let's look at the effects of strife, bitterness, anger, and resentment, and then you determine if they are worth the cost.

Strife

Strife is defined as a contention, word battle, or struggle between rivals.

> *"The beginning of strife is as when water first trickles [from a crack in a dam]; therefore stop contention before it becomes worse and quarreling breaks out."*
> Proverbs 17:14

Avoid even the initial rumbling of strife before the matter escalates into a full blown "war."

> *"He who loves strife and is quarrelsome loves transgression and involves himself in guilt."*
> Proverbs 17:19

Allowing strife into your life also invites guilt! It is a wise woman who avoids allowing herself to get entangled in the "trap" of strife.

> *It is man's honor to avoid strife, but every fool is quick to quarrel.*
> Proverbs 20:3 NIV

Anger

Anger is defined as the working and fermenting of the mind, the demonstration of strong passion, which may result in anger or revenge, though it does not necessarily include it.

> *"He who is slow to anger is better than the mighty, and he who rules his own spirit than he who takes a city."*
> Proverbs 16:32

122

"Good sense makes a man restrain his anger, and it is his glory to overlook a transgression or an offense."
Proverbs 19:11

Self-control and self-discipline are highly regarded <u>and</u> required in those who follow Jesus Christ. Self-control is wisdom and is better than being a mighty warrior.

A pattern of codependency may exist in your marriage, where you cover up, and excuse your spouse's inappropriate behaviors. The Word of God is clear that **you** are responsible for **yourself** and each person will be held accountable before the Lord on the appointed day.

You are responsible to exercise control ONLY over yourself. You are NOT responsible to control others, to control their responses or try to control the outside situation.

Sometimes wives in abusive marriages actually hinder the Lord's correction of their husband when they cover-up, excuse, or rationalize their spouses wrong behaviors.

"A man of great wrath shall suffer the penalty, for if you deliver him [from the consequences], he will [feel free to] cause you to do it again. Hear counsel, receive instruction and accept correction, that you may be wise in the time to come."
Proverbs 19:19,20

Pursue Peace

Peace is defined as the contrast of strife, a state of health or well-being; a state of untroubled, undisturbed well being, and an absence of war or other hostilities.

How are you to pursue peace when it's absolutely "insane" around you or inside of you?

The devil's plan is to bring strife into your life and house. He will daily present opportunities for your feelings to become "bruised" <u>and</u> for you to take offense! **You** are the one who always has the choice of responding POSITIVELY or NEGATIVELY! You must know that satan's agenda is to steal peace and cause strife within you **and** between you and others! Jesus Christ came to overcome satan, so you can call upon Him and enjoy peace even in the **midst of your daily life storms!**

> *"Peace I leave with you; My [own] peace I now give and bequeath to you. Not as the world gives do I give to you. Do not let your heart be troubled, neither let it be afraid—<u>stop allowing yourselves to be agitated and disturbed;</u> and do not permit yourselves to be fearful and intimidated and cowardly and unsettled."*
> John 14:27

God's plan and desire is for you to make a determined choice to live in peace with Him, with yourself, and others. We are to pursue peace with a "burning passion" (1 Peter 3:10,11).

One of the best ways you can pursue peace is to avoid "word battles" and "silly" conversations.

> *"But refuse—shut your mind against, have nothing to do with—trifling (ill-informed, unedifying, stupid) controversies over ignorant questionings, for you know that they foster strife and breed quarrels.*
>
> *And the servant of the Lord must not be quarrelsome— fighting and contending. Instead he must be kindly to every one and mild-tempered—preserving the bond of peace..."*
> 2 Timothy 2:23,24

Hebrews 12:14,15 instructs us to "strive to live in peace with everyone and to seek a holy life so you may see the Lord." It also forewarns us to be on the watch... "in order that no root of resentment (rancor, bitterness, or hatred) shoot forth causing trouble and bitter torment," which ultimately will contaminate or defile your life.

Your Inner Battle Zone

Are you **angry** with God? Are you angry with yourself?

Are you **striving** with God? Are you striving with yourself?

> *"Don't grieve God. Don't break his heart. His Holy Spirit, moving and breathing in you, is the most intimate part of your life, making you fit for himself. Don't take such a gift for granted."*
> Ephesians 4:30 MSG

Two things happen when you allow this battle to silently rage on inside you:

- It saddens and grieves the heart of God.

- It creates guilt and condemnation in your heart consequently hindering your confidence to rightfully approach God.

> *"My dear children, let's not just talk about love; let's practice real love. This is the only way we'll know we're living truly, living in God's reality. It's also the way to shut down debilitating self-criticism, even when there is something to it. For God is greater than our worried hearts and knows more about us than we do ourselves.*
>
> *And friends, <u>once that's taken care of and we're no longer accusing or condemning ourselves, we're bold and free before God!</u> We're able to stretch our hands out and receive what we asked for because we're doing what he said, doing what pleases him."*
> I John 3:18-22 MSG

Today, Jesus Christ wants **to liberate you**, bring you an answer of peace and open the door to an intimate relationship with Him!

Will you allow Him? Will you cooperate by giving Him your pain, anger and disappointments? Ask the Holy Spirit to help you release your anger and strife. He will tenderly walk you through the process and set you free today!

You are not alone! Boldly call on Jesus Christ!

As you start applying these newly discovered truths, just know you can <u>boldly</u> call on Jesus Christ! He wants you to come to His throne of grace. He will give you <u>His</u> patience and <u>His</u> peace to continue onward in addressing your relationships.

> *"Let us then fearlessly and confidently and boldly draw near to the throne of grace—the throne of God's unmerited favor [to us sinners]; that we may receive mercy [for our failures] and find grace to help in good time for every need—appropriate help and well-timed help, <u>coming just when we need it.</u>"*
> Hebrews 4:16

Life is truly easier when we choose to live right AND actively pursue peace with everyone!

> *"I have told you these things so that in Me you may have perfect peace and confidence. In the world you have tribulation and trials and distress and frustration; but be of good cheer— take courage, be confident, certain, undaunted—for I have overcome the world.—I have deprived it of power to harm, have conquered it [for you.]"*
> John 16:33

Quality Choice:

With the help of the Holy Spirit decide to daily renew your mind! God desires for you to live a life of freedom. He wants you to experience His righteousness, peace, and joy!

Prescription 7

1. As a child of God you have His divine nature within you. You have the ability to be "slow to anger" as your Heavenly Father. **Psalms 103:8; 2 Peter 1:4**

2. The strong and honorable person will control their temper. **Proverbs 16:32**

3. Strife stems from pride and spiritual immaturity. Strife is to be avoided at all costs. **I Corinthians 3:3; Philippians 2:3; I Timothy 6:4**

4. Jesus Christ gave you His "perfect peace" to allow you to overcome the storms of life. **John 14:27**

5. You are to pursue peace at all costs. **Romans 12:18; 1 Peter 3:10**

6. Continue reading statements 74-85 in Chapter 25 <u>My Daily Confessions</u>.

Practical Exercises

✔ How are we to clothe ourselves each day? (Romans 13:3)

✔ How do we avoid arguments? (Proverbs 25:15; Proverbs 15:1)

✔ When shall we see the Lord? (Hebrews 12:14,15)

✔ What happens when I choose to use the wisdom from above? (James 3:17,18)

✔ See the book "Deadly Emotions" by Dr. Don Colbert.

✔ Ask the Holy Spirit to help you identify the records of anger, bitterness, strife or resentment you are holding in your heart against yourself and others. Record (confess) these instances in a notebook. Upon completion of logging the offenses:

  • Close the notebook and seal it with tape.

  • In a private and quiet place, lift up the notebook. Now make a willful choice to release the entire contents of the notebook to God!

  • After you have released the contents to God, promptly destroy the notebook!

    "Purify me with hyssop, and I shall be clean [ceremonially]; wash me, and I shall [in reality] be whiter than snow." Psalms 51:7

20

Key 8: God-Confident to Be Different — Allow the True You to Stand Up!

One of the "stumbling blocks" within an abusive marriage is losing your identity. You begin to morph, change, and numb yourself over and over to gain your spouse's acceptance. One day I realized I had altered my personality to the degree that I was losing the true connection I had with myself.

My personality is normally outgoing, bubbly, and enjoys interacting with people. As our marital relationship further deteriorated, my personality became somber and I sought solitude. I wanted my spouse to shine when we were around others and I forced myself to be quiet so he would approve.

One day, during the final stages of our separation, I looked in the mirror and realized I didn't recognize myself. The face staring back in the mirror barely resembled the true me. I had lost, or to be exact, given up my self-confidence for the sake of someone else's approval.

Another "stumbling block" I tripped over was comparing my life and marriage (or quality of the marriage) to other marriages around me. Now isn't that just silly? I compared my marriage to marriages of those in our church, our neighborhood, and our workplaces, yet all the while, my flawed thinking made me more depressed and upset with myself.

With much prayer and reading, the Lord revealed, "Michele, **I** formed, made, and created you for **My** glory. It is **unwise** for you to compare yourself with anyone else. I've made you unique unto myself!" It was at that moment that I realized I had allowed myself to be deceived by my own misconception of others!

Wow! What a burden lifter!

> *"Not that we [have the audacity to] venture to class or [even
> to] compare ourselves with some who exalt and furnish
> testimonials for themselves! However, when they measure
> themselves with themselves and compare themselves with one
> another, <u>they are without understanding and behave
> unwisely</u>."*
> 2 Corinthians 10:12

God chose me out of love as recorded in Ephesians 1:4-6. God formed, made, and created me solely for His glory (Isaiah 43:7).

He designed me with a specific plan and purpose in mind, one, which only I can fill (Romans 12:5-8).

He intentionally made each of us distinctly different and unique as a glory and honor unto Him. The same manner in which He gave different splendor to the sun, moon, and each of the stars is the same care He took in making **you** unique (I Corinthians 15:41)!

By perfectly planned design He made each of us as a "custom creation," a "one-of-a-kind original masterpiece." You possess your own DNA structure, retinal pattern, fingerprints, voice pattern, specific talents, abilities, and unique appearance.

God desires to radiate His love through your unique personality so His glory may be seen in this world (1 Peter 1:23).

> *"May He grant you out of the rich treasury of His glory to
> be strengthened and reinforced with mighty power in the
> inner man by the (Holy) Spirit [Himself]—<u>indwelling your
> innermost being and personality</u>."*
> Ephesians 3:16

He has made you accepted and beloved in His sight. I needed to learn to accept myself again. "If God is for me who can be against me?"

Here's a sobering question, since God loves you, uniquely formed and created you for His glory: do you have a right to <u>not</u> accept yourself? The answer is **NO!**

God asks, who are you to question Him about the manner in which He designed you? (Isaiah 45:9-12)

Even the Apostle Paul learned not to judge himself NOR allow the words of others to judge him. You too must choose not to allow yourself to think or speak negatively of yourself or to become affected by the words of others. When I finally grabbed onto this truth, "the window of my mind" was opened and a fresh gust of air blew through.

I have since learned to be God-confident **NOT** self-confident! As I continue accepting the depth of God's love for me, the time He spent in uniquely creating me and for sending His Son to shed His blood for me on Calvary, the best thing I can do is to learn to recognize and appreciate my unique God given design. Jesus Christ is not ashamed of you, so why should you allow yourself to be full of shame?

Learn to accept God's love, learn to accept yourself and appreciate your God given uniqueness!

Some other truths to realize in self-acceptance include:

- You are an individual member of the Body of Christ with your own place and function SPECIFICALLY assigned by God.

- God gave you unique gifts, talents, and abilities for HIS glory!

- God gave you gifts, talents, and abilities to use in building up and serving the Body of Christ.

- It's FOOLISH and a waste of your time to compare yourself to others—to be envious or jealous of another's uniqueness.

- God handpicked YOU to be His child.

- God, your Heavenly Father, and His Son Jesus Christ are NOT ashamed of you. Why be ashamed of yourself by wishing you were someone else?

- God has a tailor made purpose for your life which only YOU can fulfill on this earth!

It's time to "shake off" the lies and misconceptions you've had about yourself. Make a choice to release your "limitations" to God. Don't dwell on them, but instead choose to work on your talents. God intentionally made you unique. Now it's up to you to discover and to celebrate those qualities by beginning to accept yourself!

Quality Choice:

Choose today to begin appreciating and then celebrating **your God given uniqueness!** Ask God to help you discover the distinct talents and abilities that He already placed inside of you. Once you have begun discovering them, begin *EXERCISING* them, and *USING* them to bless the lives of others. Remember, He made you to bring glory to Himself.

Prescription 8

1. God specifically formed, made, and created YOU for His glory. **Isaiah 43:7**

2. God chose you as His child before He formed the world and He preplanned a good path for your life. You are well pleasing in His sight. **Ephesians 1:4-6**

3. God gave you unique talents, gifts, and abilities to bring Him glory. You will ONLY find genuine life fulfillment as you use those gifts for Him. **Romans 12:5-8**

4. God intentionally made you unique. You are not to resemble or imitate anyone else on this earth. He wants you to accept your uniqueness. **Romans 9:20-23; Isaiah 45:9-12**

5. You do not have a right to judge or discredit yourself. Jesus Christ has made you righteous, free of guilt, free of shortcomings, and condemnation. He is <u>not</u> ashamed of you. **I Corinthians 4:3-5; Hebrews 2:11**

Practical Exercises

✔ List ten traits, skills, talents, and/or features that make you unique. (Where do you naturally excel? What delights you? What dreams are planted inside of you?)

✔ How are we to govern our choices in this life? (Galatians 5:24-26)

✔ Why did God form you and make you? (Isaiah 43:7)

✔ What was God's reason for picking you as His child? (Ephesians 1:4-6)

✔ Is Jesus Christ ashamed of you? (Hebrews 12:11)

✔ Instead of focusing on your limitations, where should your eyes be focused? (Hebrews 12:1-3)

✔ See the "Color Code" book by Dr. Taylor Hartman to determine your basic personality profile.

✔ Ask the Holy Spirit to help you identify the current areas of your basic personality that **He wants to help change, into the personality of Jesus Christ!**

21

Key 9: Friends versus Associates: Do You Know the Difference?

Have you heard the old saying, "Birds of a feather flock together?" Well it's true, the caliber of the people in your inner circle of relationships determine the quality of our life. Your associates have the ability to promote or hinder your mental, emotional and spiritual health.

You can choose to fly with eagles; or chickens, vultures or turkeys. It's ultimately your choice!

> *"Do not be so deceived and misled! Evil companionships
> (communion, associations) corrupt and deprave good
> manners and morals and character."*
> I Corinthians 15:33

Taking stock of the character of the people in your "inner" circle, those from whom you take advice, is extremely crucial at this time in your life. Having positive companions and counsel within your "inner" circle cannot be overstated enough.

While going through my multiple separations and ultimately divorce, I realized I had allowed several groups of individuals to "influence" me. Each group proactively wanted to "give me counsel." They included:

- Those who consistently disparaged my spouse and encouraged me to leave him while recounting their own former pains of a "failed" marriage. Unfortunately they spoke out of their own brokenness and unresolved past hurts.

- Those who held a judgmental/self righteous attitude because they didn't understand the dynamics of domestic abuse. They frequently questioned whether or not I had sought the Lord before making choices related to my marriage.

- Those who shared secular views concerning the matter of separation. Their perception encouraged women to become embittered, to retaliate, and give the cold shoulder to their spouse. This was another unsuitable response for me.

- Finally, mature Christians who non-judgmentally counseled me by offering a listening ear, supportive prayers for wisdom and strength from the Lord. They ultimately encouraged me to become the best person I could be during the midst of the most challenging season in my life.

Their prayers and Godly words gave me the boost I needed to keep seeking the Lord and to not turn my back on Him in my dire time of need. Overall this group of people helped me draw closer to God. Over the years, I've learned there is safety in **wise** counsel.

Get honest with yourself and assess, who is in your inner circle. What words of advice are they offering you? Do their words bring peace or confusion? Do their words drive you closer to the presence of God or away from Him?

Psalms 1:1,2 advises us to seek Godly counsel and to avoid ungodly counsel at all costs.

Today I thank the Lord for each of those men and women. Their words helped save my mental health and my very life (Proverbs 11:14). Yet here's the balance: Godly friends are priceless when it comes to encouraging and comforting you. *But ultimately, the sole responsibility of your choice rests between you and the Lord.* Your relationship with Him can become the most intimate you will ever know when you choose to pour out your heart with its good, bad, and ugly concerns at the throne of Jesus Christ.

Your life is valuable to Christ. Choose Godly friendships that will encourage your spiritual character to mature in Him. A Godly and genuine relationship is a MUTUAL relationship without selfishness or the intention to use someone else for personal gain.

Examples of Godly Friendships (Covenant Relationship)

Wise friendships, as recorded in the Bible, were not as casually entered into as they are today. Individuals took time, choosing people who would make them better as individuals and they took an oath to protect and honor one another.

It was a covenant relationship, one defined as "a pledge, oath, standing contract between two parties," typically ratified by the shedding of blood. That which belonged to one individual now also belonged to the other individual. It was a vow to honor and protect the other. If you failed to live up to your vow, the penalty was death.

David and Jonathan (I Samuel 18:1-4; 19:1-7; 20:1-4,12-16) Their relationship was characterized by mutual respect, brotherly love, loyalty to the truth, and mutual disclosure.

Abraham and God (James 2:23; Isaiah 41:8; Genesis 15:18; Genesis 18:16-33) Their relationship was characterized by mutual respect, open communication, care, and trust.

Learn how to make Godly friendships from these recorded relationships.

Become Selective About Your Inner Circle

"Be well-balanced—temperate, sober-minded; be vigilant and cautious at all times, for that enemy of yours, the devil, roams around like a lion roaring [in fierce hunger], seeking someone to seize upon and devour."
1 Peter 5:8

"Do not be misled: Bad company corrupts good character."
1 Corinthians 15:33 NIV

God has a good plan for your life that can only be hindered by your unbelief **or** by your dreams being "devoured" by those **you choose** to place in your circle of friends. In an attempt to detract you from the destiny and vision God is placing within your heart, one of satan's tactics includes using the people CLOSEST to you to "dampen or douse" your passion for the goal.

Realize your life is invaluable to God. Become selective in the choice of people you allow into your "inner circle" of friends. Based upon instances recorded in the Scriptures, listed below are types of people that can short circuit God's good plan for your life:

- Those who focus on your past
- Those who focus on your "limitations"
- Those who feed your "weaknesses"
- Those who cause you to rebel against God
- Those who feed your "greed" or "discontent"
- Those who trivialize your God given passion (Stay away from those who want to "douse" your destiny)
- Those who think you are "unworthy" of achieving God's goal for your life
- Those who refuse to defend you in your absence
- Those who slander or undermine your character
- Those who feed your doubt, worry and fear further causing you to not believe God's destiny for your life

Jesus - A Man, Free of People Pleasing!

> *"Think of yourselves the way Christ Jesus thought of himself."*
> Philippians 2:5 MSG

Let us each learn to become like Jesus Christ. He lived free of "co-dependency" and the fear of rejection from others. He never determined his actions or reactions based upon the behaviors of others. His sole motive was to please the Heavenly Father (John 5:30)!

Jesus Christ lived:

- *Independent* of man's opinion (John 2:24)
- *Dependent* upon God (John 5:10; John 8:29; I Peter 2:23)
- *Codependent* - Never! (Matthew 22:16)

Upon entering a relationship with God through Jesus Christ, God designed for us to be directed by the Scriptures and the Holy Spirit for day to day living. We are not to determine our actions and responses based upon others' opinions.

"The fear of human opinion disables; trusting in God protects you from that."
Proverbs 29:25 MSG

"Now am I trying to win the favor of men, or of God? Do I seek to be a man-pleaser? If I were still seeking popularity with men, I should not be a bondservant of Christ, the Messiah."
Galatians 1:10

The Apostle Paul shares that he would be an unqualified servant of Christ if he chose "public opinion" over the leading of Jesus Christ.

Following people will make you unstable, unpredictable, and miserable. Ultimately this is displeasing to God (Romans 8:6; Galatians 6:8). Following the Holy Spirit will bring you peace, freedom and joy. Making this choice **is** pleasing to God (Romans 8:6; Acts 5:29; 1 Thessalonians 2:4).

As you become more intimate with Christ—motivated by His ways and making choices, as He would direct, you will become **FREE** of the bondage of codependency!

Quality Choice:

Choose to seek out and associate with people who will speak words of *life* to you and about you; and encourage/challenge you to mature in your walk with Jesus Christ.

Ask the Holy Spirit to direct you to Christ-centered relationships. As you choose wisely the Lord will honor you. (Psalms 45:7)

Prescription 9

1. Friendships with foolish people will destroy you. **Proverbs 13:20; I Corinthians 5:9-11**

2. True friends will not gossip. **Proverbs 17:9**

3. Avoid making friends with angry "driven" people. **Proverbs 22:24**

4. To make good friends, you must first be a good friend. **Proverbs 17:17; Proverbs 18:24**

5. Advice from a true friend will cheer you up and make you stronger. **Psalms 133:1,3; Proverbs 27:9,17**

Practical Exercises

✔ How did Jesus Christ demonstrate His friendship to you? (John 15:13-20)

✔ What happens to you when you choose quality friends? (Proverbs 27:17)

✔ How can you distinguish a genuine (spiritual) person from a carnal Christian? (Matthew 12:33-37; Luke 6:43-45)

✔ Is it possible to be friends with the world and friends with God? (James 4:4)

22

Key 10: Hold Fast! Determine to Continue in the Truth

Congratulate yourself! While discovering each key, you have made much personal progress! Continue applying the quality choices as they are revealed in your life—one by one. This requires a focused and committed effort. If you're an "achiever" by nature, please be patient with yourself! If you are "self-critical" by nature, please learn to extend mercy to yourself!

You are encouraged to hold fast to that which is "proven and good." Hold fast, means grasp firmly, <u>not</u> relaxing your grip. God promises to be faithful to His Word in your life through the return of Jesus Christ. Today, <u>you</u> must be the one to determine to be faithful to Him!

> *"But test and prove all things [until you can recognize] what is good; [to that] hold fast.*
>
> *Abstain from evil—shrink from it and keep aloof from it—in whatever form or whatever kind it may be.*
>
> *And may the God of peace Himself sanctify you through and through—that is, separate you from profane things, make you pure and wholly consecrated to God—and may your spirit and soul and body be preserved sound and complete [and found] blameless at the coming of our Lord Jesus Christ, the Messiah."*
> I Thessalonians 5:21-23

Determine today to avoid a "defeatist" attitude. Stay focused in doing good (making quality choices from the Word of God) and your diligence will be rewarded.

"And let us not lose heart and grow weary and faint in acting nobly and doing right, for in due time and at the appointed season we shall reap, if we do not loosen and relax our courage and faint."
Galatians 6:9

Once you have found the truth and been set free, INSANITY is returning to the same old thing (old behaviors, old mindsets, old ways of speaking) yet expecting different results!

God's Word IS <u>the final authority</u>! It alone sets the standard for life and what God defines as normal. Anything contradictory to the Word of God is substandard, abnormal, and ABUSIVE (not the use of His original intention).

What and Why Should I Hold Fast?

- Hold fast with the confidence that Jesus Christ will always be with you. Continue looking to Him for direction. You are to hold fast, firm, and unshaken to the end.

    "For we have become fellows with Christ, the Messiah, and share in all He has for us, if only we hold our first newborn confidence and original assured expectation [in virtue of which we are believers] firm and unshaken <u>to the end.</u>"
    Hebrews 3:14

- Hold fast to the truth you have discovered and now believe about Jesus Christ! He came to set you free and give you the tools to be an overcomer in this world! Hold fast in what you confess about Jesus Christ because He is your High Priest who understands everything you will ever encounter. He wants you to come boldly to His throne for any and all of your needs!

    "So let us seize and hold fast and retain without wavering <u>the hope we cherish and confess</u>, and our acknowledgement of it, for He Who promised is reliable (sure) and faithful to His Word."
    Hebrews 10:23

- Holding fast to the revealed truths brings you eternal rewards and recognition from Jesus Christ, the Messiah. Hold fast to what you have discovered and seen from the Scriptures.

> *"Only hold fast to what you have until I come.*
>
> *And he who overcomes (is victorious) and who obeys My commands to the [very] end— doing the works [that please Me]—I will give him authority and power over the nations;*
>
> *And he shall rule them with a scepter (rod) of iron, as when earthen pots are broken in pieces, and [his power over them shall be] like that which I Myself have received from My Father."*
> Revelation 2:25-27

- Holding fast, continuing in His Word for your daily living shows you are a <u>true</u> follower (disciple, disciplined one) in Jesus Christ. By continuing in His Word and applying it's truths, you will continue to be set FREE!

> *"So Jesus said to those Jews who had believed in Him, If you abide in My Word—hold fast to My teachings and live in accordance with them—you are truly My disciples.*
>
> *And you will know the truth, and the truth will set you free."*
> John 8:31,32

You Now Know the Secret; You Are Not Alone!

Learn the secret of running YOUR life's race with success! Your true strength and endurance lies in Jesus Christ! Stay tapped into Him and His Word for your life so you may finish strong across *your* finish line.

During life's trials and seasons of growth, the Scriptures instruct you to be patient. Patience is NOT the ability "to wait." It is the ability to keep the right attitude while you are waiting and holding fast to

Scriptural truth. Patience is a fruit of the Spirit that can be defined as "the ability to bear trials without grumbling."

God designed you to walk by faith (His Word) NOT by your feelings and emotions. Walking by the Spirit, His revealed Word, IS THE WAY OF LIFE. The rewards of walking by the Spirit include gaining spiritual maturity and enjoying personal life fulfillment!

So, hold fast to your confidence in Jesus Christ and hold fast to _His_ identity of you until He returns. This is a daily choice.

Here's a Comforting Reminder: You Are a Masterpiece in Progress!

Jesus Christ is by your side walking you step-by-step in each growth area of your life. Jesus Christ is the AUTHOR and FINISHER of your faith. His goal is to progressively change you from one degree of glory (healing and growth) to the next degree of glory.

Realize you are a constant work in progress until Jesus Christ returns. In the meantime, be patient with yourself! Stay receptive and He will successfully keep guiding you through the process into the destiny He purposed for your life!

Quality Choice:

Choose the way of the Spirit as revealed in the written Scriptures. You will find FREEDOM and genuine strength only through Jesus Christ. Hold fast to the truth with patience and He will carry you through to your finish line!

Prescription 10

1. Not believing in the truth of God's Word brings bondage into your life and hinders you from receiving the promises of God. **Hebrews 3:7-13**

2. God guarantees that you will reap benefits in your life by holding fast to the truth. **Galatians 6:7-9**

3. Deciding to "let go" of the truth after you have discovered it brings sin into your life. **James 4:17**

4. You are to hold fast to the truth of Christ and His wholesome, sound teaching for your life. **2 Timothy 1:13; Hebrews 4:14**

5. Complete reading statements 86-100 in Chapter 25 <u>My Daily Confessions</u>.

Practical Exercises

✔ What is the race you are in as a Christian? (I Corinthians 9:24-27)

✔ What are the benefits of staying faithful to the Word of God? (John 8:31,32; Revelation 2:26,27; 3:11)

✔ When will the Lord stop working with you? (Philippians 1:6)

✔ How long should you hold fast to God's Word? (Revelation 2:25; 3:3,11)

23

Key 11: It's Time to Lift Your Head!

You Belong to the God of Newness!

"Do not [earnestly] remember the former things, neither consider the things of old.

Behold, I am doing a new thing; now it springs forth; do you not perceive and know it, and will you not give heed to it? I will make a way in the wilderness and rivers in the desert."
Isaiah 43:18,19

New = Hebrew word CHALASH = New, fresh, unheard of, new in quality

God wants you to know TODAY, that He is doing a new thing in your life! He is clearing a path for you and is bringing life into a former "dead" situation. Today He is here tenderly taking and lifting your face upward into His hands.

The question is, will you cooperate with Him by walking in the NEW direction He has foreordained for your life?

When the Lord told me, "Arise, Michele, this is a new day. Lift up your head. I have taken the things of the past away!" I realized that it was up to me to cooperate with His command. On that day, I made the commitment to God that I agreed...<u>TODAY</u> is the <u>FIRST</u> day of the rest of my life! I will no longer dwell on old thoughts, memories, and regrets, but I choose **today** to step into a "new day" for the next phase of my life!

> *"<u>And I will restore or replace for you the years</u> that the locust has eaten, the hopping locust, the stripping locust, and the crawling locust, My great army which I sent among you.*

And you shall eat in plenty and be satisfied, and praise the name of the Lord, your God, Who has dealt wondrously with you. And My people shall never be put to shame."
Joel 2:25,26

From that day forward, the Lord brought a fresh wind through my soul, strengthened my heart, and set my mind free of the past. He will do the SAME for you if you will allow Him, *and* when you choose to cooperate.

Behold, He Can Make All Things New! (Will You Choose to Cooperate?)

Let's look at some of the other areas the Lord can and will make NEW when we choose to believe and follow His plan:

- The Lord has a **new name** for you. He's declaring to you today that He is the One who will protect and defend you and He is the One "married" to you.

> *"And the nations shall see your righteousness and vindication—your rightness and justice [not your own, but His ascribed to you]—and all kings shall behold your salvation and glory and you—shall be called by a new name, which the mouth of the Lord shall name.*
>
> *You shall also be [so beautiful and prosperous as to be thought of as] a crown of glory and honor in the hand of the Lord, and a royal diadem [exceedingly beautiful] in the hand of your God.*
>
> *You [Judah] shall no more be termed Forsaken, nor shall your land be called Desolate any more, but you shall be called Hephzibah [My delight is in her], and your land be called Beulah [that is, Married]; for the Lord delights in you, and your land shall be married [owned and protected by the Lord]."*
> Isaiah 62:2-4

- He desires to use your life in **new ways**. He can and will make you a "sharp new instrument, fit for His personal use." Your *true* life's purpose is to bring Him honor and glory.

> *"For I, the Lord your God, hold your right hand; I, Who say to you, Fear not, I will help you!*
>
> *Fear not, you worm Jacob, you men of Israel! I will help you, says the Lord; your Redeemer is the Holy One Of Israel.*
>
> *Behold, I will make you to be a new, sharp, threshing instrument having teeth; you shall thresh the mountains and beat them small, and shall make the hills as chaff."*
> Isaiah 41:13-15

The Lord is with you as He was with Isaiah. What is the perception that you hold of yourself? Is it God's <u>limitless</u> perspective **or** your <u>limited</u> perspective? Unlike the Israelites, declare and realize today that you are NOT a lowly "worm." Ask the Lord to open your eyes so you can see and appreciate the true strength, true power, and true worth given to you by Jesus Christ!

- The Lord places a **new song** in your mouth as you line up your words to become His Words and your thoughts to become His thoughts in your life. Others will gain reverence for God when they see and hear the change in you.

> *"And He has put a new song in my mouth, a song of praise to our God. Many shall see and fear—revere, and worship—and put their trust and confident reliance in the Lord."*
> Psalms 40:3
>
> *"I will sing a new song to You, O God; upon a harp, an instrument of ten strings, will I offer praises to You."*
> Psalms 144:9

Due to His compassion, the Lord gives you a **new start** EACH day! Why would you choose to hold onto stale, dead, or former things (old thoughts, responses, behaviors)?

> *"They are new every morning; great and abundant is Your stability and faithfulness."*
> Lamentations 3:23

- Whenever you turn to the Lord, He RESTORES your life and its quality with a **new heart** and a **new spirit**.

> *"A new heart I will give you, and a new spirit will I put within you: and I will take away the stony heart out of your flesh and give you a heart of flesh.*
>
> *And I will put my Spirit within you and cause you to walk in My statues, and you shall heed My ordinances, and do them.*
>
> *Thus says the Lord God: In the day that I cleanse you from all your iniquities I will cause [Israel's] cities to be inhabited, and <u>the waste places shall be rebuilt</u>.*
>
> *And the desolate land shall be tilled, that which had lain desolate in the sight of all who passed by.*
>
> *And they shall say, This land that was desolate has become like the garden of Eden, and the waste and desolate and ruined cities are fortified and inhabited.*
>
> *Then the nations that are left round about you shall know that I, the Lord, have rebuilt the ruined places, and replanted that which was desolate. I, the Lord, have spoken it, and I will do it."*
> Ezekiel 36:26-27,33-36

Why does He need to make you new? Because your former ways, former words and former thoughts are <u>unable</u> to withstand the powerful new nature of Jesus Christ that now lives in you!

> *"No one sews a patch of (new) unshrunken goods on an old garment; if he does, the patch tears away from it, the new from the old, and the rent becomes bigger and worse [than it is was before].*

And no one puts new wine into old wineskins; if he does, the wine will burst the skins, and the wine is lost and the bottles destroyed; but new wine is to put in new (fresh) wineskins."
Mark 2:21,22

Read Ezekiel 37:1-14 (AMP). It is the record of the "Valley of Dry Bones," which was fully restored to life! This passage shows that only the Lord can bring life from a visibly hopeless situation. The Lord can breathe NEW life into your "deadest" of situations. As described in the passage, restoration occurs in progressive stages. In the meantime, your part is to maintain a patient attitude with a Godly confession of "life-giving words" while the gradual change(s) are taking place.

As a Christian, meaning "Christ **in** You", you are not hopeless! You have an opportunity EVERY moment in life to receive a NEW start!

"I appeal to you therefore, brethren, and beg of you in view of [all] the mercies of God, to make a decisive dedication of your bodies— presenting all your members and faculties—as a living sacrifice, holy (devoted, consecrated) and well pleasing to God, which is your reasonable (rational, intelligent) service and spiritual worship.

Do not be conformed to this world—this age, fashioned after and adapted to its external, superficial customs. But be transformed (changed) by the [entire] renewal of your mind—by its new ideals and its new attitude—so that you may prove [for yourselves] what is that good and acceptable and perfect will of God, even the thing which is good and acceptable and perfect [in His sight for you]."
Romans 12:1,2

"Therefore if any person is (ingrafted) in Christ, the Messiah, he is (a new creature altogether,) a new creation; the old (previous moral and spiritual condition) has passed away. Behold, the fresh and new has come!"
2 Corinthians 5:17

Read the END of the "Owner's Manual" (the Bible). **Through Jesus Christ, you overcome, you win!**

It is NEVER too late for the Lord to give you a NEW START, a FRESH beginning! The real question is…will YOU choose to receive it?

> *"Then I saw a new sky (heaven) and a new earth; for the former sky and the former earth had passed away (vanished) and there no longer existed any sea.*
>
> *And I saw the holy city, the new Jerusalem, descending out of heaven from God, all arrayed like a bride beautiful and adorned for her husband.*
>
> *And He Who is seated on the throne said, See! I make all things new. Also He said, Record this, for these sayings are faithful—accurate, incorruptible and trustworthy—and true (genuine)."*
> Revelations 21:1,2,5

Quality Choice:

Boldly declare…"**Today** is the **first day** of the rest of my life! Today, I choose to step into the good destiny God has planned for me!"

Practical Exercise

Invite an *encouraging friend* to witness and support you in this Passage ceremony. This is a five-step process:

1. Pick a quiet spot indoors or outdoors that brings peace to you. Once there, draw a line on the ground or floor (if indoors, use tape, preferably red colored tape.) The red tape represents the blood Jesus Christ shed for your life. Where you are currently standing designates "The Past to Today," the other side of the tape designates "Today, Your New Day to the rest of your

life." Today, Jesus Christ wants to seal off your past and *move you forward* into a bright, new, expectant future!

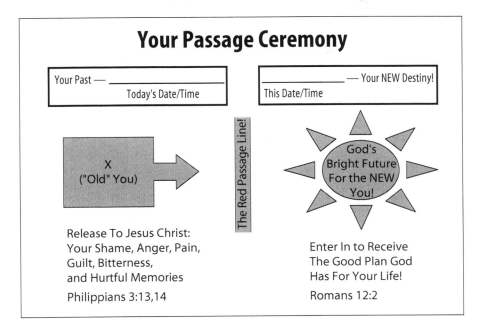

Your Passage Ceremony

Your Past — _____
          Today's Date/Time

_____ — Your NEW Destiny!
This Date/Time

The Red Passage Line!

X
("Old" You)

God's
Bright Future
For the NEW
You!

Release To Jesus Christ:
Your Shame, Anger, Pain,
Guilt, Bitterness,
and Hurtful Memories

Philippians 3:13,14

Enter In to Receive
The Good Plan God
Has For Your Life!

Romans 12:2

2. While on the current side, make a quality choice to "shed the old you" by leaving the pain, burdens, cares, and offenses of the past on THAT side of the tape. **Do not cross the line until you have determined to give everything to Jesus Christ and allow Him to care for you.**

3. Now, CROSS OVER the red line, stepping into your NEW day and the bright future of the NEW woman inside of you!

4. Determine not to look back, not to recall the things of the past, and not to live in regret.

5. Raise your hands in Victory and thankfulness to Jesus Christ for setting you free! His promise to you today is still the same **"...behold, I make all things new!"**

Your Next Steps...

Only YOU can choose to do the following:

1. Call upon God for help.

2. Acquire a revelation of your TRUE identity and worth in Christ.

3. Discover your promise in the Word of God.

4. Have faith in that promise.

5. Ask the Holy Spirit to comfort and guide you into all truth about your life. **John 14:16,17; John 16:7-13**

6. Then act on it. This is called "Believing."

7. Continue applying what the Scriptures and the Holy Spirit reveal to you.

Tip

You have read and discovered that CHOICES are POWERFUL. You have learned that right choices bring blessings while poor choices bring consequences.

A woman cannot experience newness of life or genuine transformation without a personal relationship with Jesus Christ!

Without Him your heart and negative outlook on life remain the same and you have no hope. Only the power of Christ can help you overcome your past and move you into a bright future. Without His power, you are destined to continue the same destructive behavioral patterns (Luke 1:37; Romans 12:1,2).

The Bible records that we cannot do anything from, by, or within ourselves (John 6:63, 5:19, 5:30), but ONLY by way of the Holy Spirit. We need to ask for and rely upon His assistance. This is THE WAY OF LIFE!

Your situation is NOT so hopeless and devastating that the Lord cannot pull you up and out of your personal "pit." Remember Joseph's restoration as recorded in the Book of Genesis and the Israelites in the Book of Jeremiah.

> *"For I will restore health to you, and I will heal your wounds, says the Lord; because they have called you an outcast, saying, This is Zion, whom no one seeks after and for whom no one cares!"*
> Jeremiah 30:17

> *"Behold, I am doing a new thing; now it springs forth; do you not perceive and know it, and will you not give heed to it? I will even make a way in the wilderness and rivers in the desert."*
> Isaiah 43:19

Determine today that THIS IS YOUR NEW BEGINNING. This is the first day of the rest of your life!

Now give the Word of God an exalted place in your life. Make a choice to continue to walk in His truth as the Holy Spirit and the Scriptures guide you.

You will keep changing and grow stronger as you continue choosing to apply the Word of Life. As we read earlier...you are NOT alone. The Lord is with you to bring you through to *your* personal finish line (Romans 12:1,2; Philippians 1:6; Hebrews 12:2).

Quality Choice:

Choose to CLOSE the door to *old* stuff (negative words, thoughts, destructive relationships, and responses to others). Choose NEWNESS of life and God's unique plan for you! (Jeremiah 29:11)

Practical Exercises

1. Present yourself as a LIVING sacrifice to the Lord... "burning" with the life of Christ from the inside out. Continue learning your spiritual RIGHTS and TRUE identity from the "Owner's Manual," the Word of God.

2. Ignite someone else's spiritual fire—Tell **<u>three other people</u> what the Lord has done for your life through this Interactive Guidebook.**

3. "Whatever He Says, *Do It!*" Make a quality choice to become promptly obedient to the things Jesus Christ is showing you about your life. Choose the way of life, because He wants to bless your life.

4. Live out the plan the Lord has ordained for your life. You are a GLORY unto Him when you live the life He designed for you. **Perseverance, obedience to the Lord, and fulfilling the plan of God for your life are the greatest victory you can have over satan.**

Congratulations! Press On!

"The Lord bless you and keep you; the Lord make His face shine upon you and be gracious to you; and the Lord turn His face toward you and give you peace."
Numbers 6:24

Closing Notes

25

Daily Confessions About Myself As God Declares

" Can two walk together, except they be agreed?"
Amos 3:3

God Declares My True Image Is:

(Place Your Name Here!) _____

1. I am God's *child* – John 1:12

2. I am *beloved* of God – John 3:16; Romans 1:7; 1 Thessalonians 1:4

3. I am *accepted* in the Beloved by God – Ephesians 1:6

4. I *cannot be separated from the love of God* – Romans 8:39

5. I am *Holy and without blame before Him* in love – 1 Peter 1:16; Ephesians 1:4

6. I *am God's child*, for I am born again of the incorruptible seed (sperm) of the WORD OF GOD which lives and abides FOREVER – 1 Peter 1:23

7. I am now *Body, Soul and Spirit* – 1 Thessalonians 5:23,24

8. I have a *NEW life* through Christ Jesus – Galatians 2:20; Colossians 3:2-4; 1 Peter 1:3,4

9. I am *born again* – John 3:3

10. I am *created in God's image* – Genesis 1:26,27

11. I am a *child of God* – Ephesians 1:5

12. I am a *child of Light* – Ephesians 5:8-11

13. I *possess His divine nature* (God's Nature, His Love Nature) – 1 Peter 1:23; 1 John 3:9,10; 1 Corinthians 13:4-8

14. I am *established, anointed and sealed by God* – 2 Corinthians 1:21,22

15. I am a *chosen race, priesthood, purchased person* – 1 Peter 2:9

16. I am a *citizen of heaven* – Philippians 3:20

17. I *possess the character traits of His nature* (Fruit of the Spirit) – Galatians 5:22

18. I *possess qualities of Gods divine nature* – 2 Peter 1:3-9

19. I am *knowledgeable* – 1 Corinthians 1:30

20. I am *wise* – 1 Corinthians 1:30

21. I am a *master (a conqueror)* – 1 John 5:4,5; 2 Corinthians 2:14

22. I always *triumph in Christ* – 2 Corinthians 2:14

23. I am *powerful*
    a.) Ability Power – Ephesians 3:16; 2 Corinthians 12:9; Philippians 4:13
    b.) Authority Power – Ephesians 1:19; Matthew 28:18,19; Luke 10:19

24. I am *disciplined / use self control* – 2 Timothy 1:7

25. I am *fearless* – 1 John 4:18; Hebrews 2:14,15

26. I am *very good* – Genesis 1:31

27. I am *honored* – Isaiah 43:4; 49:5

28. I am *dignified* – Psalm 103:4

29. I am *precious* – Isaiah 43:4

30. I am *sound (made whole)*
    a.) Soul – Isaiah 53:5; Colossians 1:20
    b.) Body – Isaiah 53:5; Matthew 8:17; 1 Peter 2:24

31. I am a *Son of God* – Ephesians 1:4,5; Hebrews 4:1a,3,5; Matthew 11:28,29
    - a.) Called to rest (The Father and Jesus have done all of it already)
    - b.) Called to respond (not to work) – John 6: 37,38; Romans 3:20, 28

32. I am the *Righteousness of God (Totally Accepted)* – Romans 5:1; Galatians 2:16

33. I am *FREE (in Christ) from guilt* – Ephesians 1:4; Romans 4:25; Hebrews 1:3; 1 Corinthians 1:8; Hebrews 9:14,19-22

34. I am *FREE* from condemnation – Romans 8:1

35. I am *defended by God* – Psalm 7:10; Romans 8:31-34; John 14:16; Hebrews 10:19-22

36. I am *forgiven of all my sins* and washed in Christ's Blood – Ephesians 1:7; Hebrews 9:14: Colossians 1:14; 1 John 1:9; 2:12

37. I am a *new creature* – 2 Corinthians 5:17

38. I am the *temple of the Holy Spirit* – 1 Corinthians 6:19; 3:16

39. I am *delivered from the power of darkness* and translated into God's kingdom – Colossians 1:13

40. I am *redeemed from the curse of the law* – I Peter 1:18,19; Galatians 3:13

41. I am *blessed* – Deuteronomy 28:1-14; Galatians 3:9

42. I am a *saint* – Romans 1:7; 1 Corinthians 1:2; Philippians 1:1

43. I am the *head* and not the tail – Deuteronomy 28:13

44. I am *above only* and not beneath – Deuteronomy 28:13

45. I am *His elect / His chosen one* – Colossians 3:12; Romans 8:33

46. I am *established to the end* – 1 Corinthians 1:8

47. I am *made nigh* by the Blood of Christ – Ephesians 2:13

48. I am *victorious* – Revelation 21:7

49. I am *set FREE* – John 8:31-33

50. I am *strong in the Lord* – Ephesians 6:10

51. I am *dead to sin* – Romans 6:2,11; 1 Peter 2:24

52. I am *more than a conqueror* – Romans 8:37

53. I am a *joint heir with Christ* – Romans 8:17

54. I am *sealed with the Holy Spirit of promise* – Ephesians 1:13

55. I am *in Christ Jesus by His doing* – 1 Corinthians 1:30

56. I am *complete* in Him – Colossians 2:10; 1:27

57. I am *crucified with Christ* – Galatians 2:20

58. I am *alive with Christ* – Ephesians 2:5

59. I am *reconciled to God* – 2 Corinthians 5:18

60. I am *now a minister of reconciliation for God* – 2 Corinthians 5:17-20

61. I am *qualified to share* in Christ's inheritance – Colossians 1:12

62. I am *firmly rooted, built up, established in my faith* and overflowing with gratitude – Colossians 2:7

63. I am a *fellow citizen with the saints and of the household of God* – Ephesians 2:19

64. I am *born of God* and *the evil one does not touch me* – 1 John 5:18

65. I am *overtaken with blessings* – Deuteronomy 28:2; Ephesians 1:3

66. I am *His disciple because I have love for others* – John 13:34,35

67. I am *the righteousness* of God – 2 Corinthians 5:21; 1 Peter 2:24

68. I am a *partaker* of His divine nature – 2 Peter 1:4

69. I am *called* of God – 2 Timothy 1:9

70. I am *chosen* by God – 1 Thessalonians 1:4; Ephesians 1:4; 1 Peter 2:9

71. I am an *Ambassador (representative) of Christ* – 2 Corinthians 5:20

72. I am *God's co-worker*- 2 Corinthians 6:1

73. I am *God's workmanship* created in Christ Jesus for good works – Ephesians 2:10

74. I am *the apple of My Heavenly Father's eye* – Deuteronomy 32:10; Psalm 17:8

75. I am *healed* by the stripes of JESUS – 1 Peter 2:24; Isaiah 53:5,6

76. I am *being changed* into His image – 2 Corinthians 3:18; Philippians 1:6

77. I am *an OVERCOMER in Christ* – John 16:33; Matthew 16:18 NIV; Luke 10:19 NIV; Romans 12:21

78. I am raised up with Christ and *seated in heavenly places* – Colossians 2:12; Ephesians 2:6

79. I have *the mind of Christ* – Philippians 2:5; 1 Corinthians 2:16; 2 Timothy 1:7

80. I have *obtained an inheritance* – Ephesians 1:11

81. I can *find grace and mercy in time of need* – Hebrews 4:16

82. I have *access* by one Spirit *unto the FATHER* – Ephesians 2:18

83. I have *overcome the world* – 1 John 5:4

84. I have *everlasting life and will not be condemned* – John. 5:24 NIV; John 6:47

85. I have *the peace of God* which passes understanding – Philippians 4:7

86. I have *received power*, the power of the Holy Spirit; power to lay hands on the sick and see them recover; power to cast out demons; power over all the power of the enemy and nothing shall by any means hurt me – Mark 16:17,18b; Luke 10:17,19

87. I *live by* and in the law of *the Spirit of Life in Christ Jesus* – Romans 8:2

88. I have *dominion over sin* in Christ Jesus – Romans 6:13,14,17,18,22

89. I *walk in Christ Jesus* – Colossians 2:6

90. I *can do all things* in Christ Jesus – Philippians 4:13

91. I shall *do even greater works* than Christ Jesus – John 14:12

92. I possess the Greatest One *in me* because greater is He who is in me than he who is in the world – 1 John 4:4

93. I *show forth His praise* – 1 Peter 2:9

94. My *life is hid with Christ in God* – Colossians 3:3

95. I am *assured all things work together for good* – Romans 8:28

96. I am *confident that the good work God begun in me will be perfected* – Philippians 1:6

97. I am *pressing toward the mark for the prize of the high calling* of Jesus Christ – Philippians 3:14

98. I am *formed, made and created for God's glory* – Isaiah 43:7

99. I have *a God ordained purpose* on this earth – Romans 8:28; 9:17; 2 Timothy 1:9

100. I have *an intimate relationship with Christ and respond to His voice* – Revelations 3:20,21

26

Your Wake-Up Call! Redeeming the Time

"Yet you do not know [the least thing] about what may happen tomorrow. What is the nature of your life? You are [really] but a wisp of vapor—a puff of smoke, a mist—that is visible for a little while and then disappears [into thin air]."
James 4:14

"Therefore He says, Awake, O sleeper, and arise from the dead, and Christ shall shine [make day dawn] upon you and give you light.

Look carefully then how you walk! Live purposefully and worthily and accurately, not as the unwise and witless, but as wise,—sensible, intelligent people;

Making the very most of the time—buying up each opportunity—because the days are evil.

<u>*Therefore do not be vague and thoughtless and foolish, but understanding and firmly grasping what the will of the Lord is.*</u>*"*
Ephesians 5:14-17

This is **YOUR** wake up call! As a woman of God with the Spirit of Christ inside of you, TIME is your most precious commodity. The minutes ticking by cannot be replaced, so **choose to use your remaining time allotment wisely!**

From God's perspective your allotted time on earth is a "vapor," a passing mist in comparison to your <u>eternal</u> destiny.

You cannot afford to be distracted by wasting your valuable time on any activities, behaviors, energies, or unhealthy relationships that in the long run will not produce good fruit **or** eternal rewards from Christ.

167

With the help of the Holy Spirit, only you can make the choice for true change! You are the only one who can determine today, "Yes, my life is important!" Carrying around emotional poison, anger, and bitterness will only hinder God's destination for your life.

The Lord has a good plan and a specific assignment for your life on this earth. You will only experience true fulfillment when you begin discovering the destiny God has planned for your life! Spend time with Him, follow His instruction and He will lead you into your specific purpose on this earth.

In Jesus Christ you will find guidance, strength, comfort, and hope! Yet **you** must choose to cooperate and follow His direction.

> *"I call Heaven and earth to witness this day against you, that I have set before you life and death, the blessings and the curses; therefore choose life, that you and your descendants may live."*
> Deuteronomy 30:19

Make a quality decision **today**...

> *"So if the Son sets you free, you will be free indeed."*
> John 8:36

Choose **His** way of life...

It's *Time* to answer His call, you *ARE* free!

27

Your Personal Invitation

You are not alone!

There is a man who wants to come alongside you for all the days of your life. A man who can fulfill your every need and longing. A man who will set your heart, soul, and mind absolutely FREE!

Will you choose to allow Him to enter into your life? **He is the man Jesus Christ!** He is the King Of Kings, Lord of Lords, and the Messiah.

Jesus Christ wants to be the lover of your soul, your companion, your husband, your most intimate friend, and closer than your very breath.

If you do not know or have a personal relationship with Jesus Christ, He invites you to do the following:

> *"That if you confess with your mouth Jesus as Lord, and believe in your heart that God raised Him from the dead, you shall be saved;*
>
> *for with the heart man believes, resulting in righteousness, and with the mouth he confesses, resulting in salvation."*
> Romans 10:9,10 NAS

If you have fallen away from your relationship with Jesus Christ and you genuinely desire to renew it, then ask for His forgiveness today. He will restore your relationship by making it brand new!

> *"If we confess our sins, He is faithful and righteous to forgive us our sins and to cleanse us from all unrighteousness."*
> I John 1:9 NAS

Amen.

28

Suggested Reading Materials

Chapter

29

Domestic Violence Contacts

Websites

Center For Prevention of Sexual & Domestic Violence
www.cpsdv.org

Families Against Violence
www.famvi.com

Time To Fly Foundation
www.timetofly.org

E-mail/Phone Contacts

Time To Fly Foundation
877-887-9386
ttfmoreinfo@timetofly.org

National Domestic Violence Hotline
(800) 799-SAFE (voice) or (800) 787-3224 (TDD)

30

Bibliography

Chapter 5

Wilson, William. *Old Testament Word Studies*. Kregal Publications, 1980, 3rd Printing.

Chapter 6

Bullinger, E.W. *A Critical Lexicon and Concordance to the English and Greek New Testament*. Zondervan Publishing House, 1975.

Chapter 11

Youssef, Michael Ph.D. *Know Your Real Enemy*. Thomas Nelson Publishing, 1997.

Chapter 13

Wilson, William. *Old Testament Word Studies*. Kregal Publications, 1980, 3rd Printing.

Chapter 16

Youssef, Michael Ph.D. *Know Your Real Enemy*. Thomas Nelson Publishing, 1997.

Chapter 17

The American Heritage Dictionary, New 2nd College Edition. Dell Publishing Company/Houghton Mifflin Company, 1983.

ABOUT THE AUTHOR

Michele is well aware of the unique needs of a hurting woman and her challenging search for effective tools to advance into a victorious life!

After personally being healed from an emotionally abusive marital relationship, she resigned as a senior professional in Corporate America to answer the call of sharing Christ's liberating truth to hurting women. Her heart's passion is directing hurting women into their God-given FREEDOM (mentally, emotionally, socially, and spiritually).

In the past twenty years, she has held key positions with various Fortune 100 companies. Her background includes corporate sales, designing training programs, serving as committee chairperson on civic and professional associations, working as Women's Bible Study Coordinator for over 15 years, and serving as a Women's Shelter Volunteer.

Michele speaks on radio, television, and at women's conferences teaching proven keys to overcome the devastation of generational domestic abuse.

To share your personal victories from this Interactive Guidebook or to request Michele to speak to your group you may contact us via:

Email: ianswered@mrjonesllc.com

Mail: MRJ / I Answered
P.O. Box 8551
Reston, VA 20195

My Journey Notes

My Journey Notes

My Journey Notes

My Journey Notes

My Journey Notes